One Man's Story

One Man's Story

Fredrik A. Schiotz

AUGSBURG Publishing House • Minneapolis

ONE MAN'S STORY

Library of Congress Catalog Card No. 80-67790

International Standard Book No. 0-8066-1851-5

MANUFACTURED IN THE UNITED STATES OF AMERICA

The Board of Publication of The American Lutheran Church, commonly known as Augsburg Publishing House, is pleased to send a copy of *One Man's Story* to all clergy of The American Lutheran Church. The emphasis of the book is on events in the life of the church and issues in the church's mission, with illustrations from the life and ministry of the ALC's first president, Dr. Fredrik A. Schiotz. May the book enrich your ministry and your understanding of the church in which you serve.

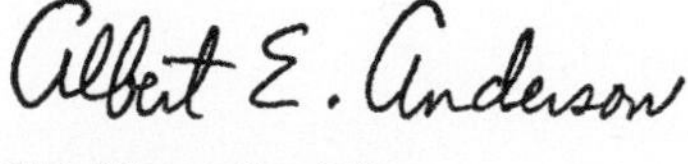

Chief Executive Officer
AUGSBURG PUBLISHING HOUSE
426 South Fifth Street
Minneapolis, MN 55415

September 1980

Contents

About This Book

I think it was about a year after I retired that Dr. Albert E. Anderson, general manager of Augsburg Publishing House, came to me and said: "You should begin to think about recording for the church the story of your life. We allowed your predecessors to die without getting a line from them!"

"Do you want a biography, or something about experiences in the service of the church?" I replied.

He answered: "Tell the story of your life, beginning with childhood and coming down through the years!"

I began to reflect about Anderson's request and to make notes. This was followed by some writing. In consultation with several advisors, including Alvin Rogness, Lily Gyldenvand, Omar Bonderud, and Roland Seboldt, the objective of the book emerged. Rather than a formal autobiography, we agreed that the emphasis was to be on events in the life of the church and issues embedded in the church's mission with the use of illustrations culled from my life and ministry. However, some biographical facts have been included that readers may recognize the forces that shaped me and controlled my decision making.

I am thankful for the opportunities the Lord has given me to serve him. To God be the glory!

Fredrik A. Schiotz

About the Author

If the church had been able to send new missionaries into China in 1930, Fredrik A. Schiotz and his ebullient wife, Dagny, would not have gone to Duluth, Minnesota. Upon receiving a call from Zion Lutheran Church, he was ordained, and thus a career was launched that in the next 40 years was to involve him in almost every area of the church's life, and make him one of the notable leaders of his generation. From a day when he was nine years old, he had felt drawn to the ministry as a calling, whether as pastor or missionary.

When at 29 he came to Duluth, the finger of leadership had already touched him. At St. Olaf College he was a member of the student senate. He was sent as a delegate to an inter-Lutheran collegiate student gathering and was elected the first president of the newly formed Lutheran Student Association of America. After graduating with honors, he interrupted his formal studies with two years of high school teaching before entering Luther Theological Seminary, St. Paul, Minnesota, in 1926.

While at the seminary again his studies were broken by a year of service as traveling secretary for the Student Volunteer Movement for Foreign Missions, one of the great stirrings among Christian students in the first half of our century. He later served on its board of directors.

After but two years in Duluth, he became pastor of Trinity, Moorhead, Minnesota, the church home of students and faculty from Concordia College and Moorhead State Teachers College. It was while here that the opportunity came for him to take a leave of absence and for a year fulfill a dream to visit the foreign mission work of his church throughout the world.

He was destined not to settle long in one place. When he had served Trinity six years, the five Lutheran bodies of the then American Lutheran Conference insisted that they had to have his services to launch a work among Lutheran students on campuses other than the church's schools. Seven years later he resigned, convinced that the time had come for the work to be transferred to the larger base of the National Lutheran Council. He then became pastor of Trinity Lutheran Church in Brooklyn, where he served for three years.

World War II had left many fields of world missions in crisis. Support from European countries had been severely curtailed, and the postwar realignments of national sovereignties in many countries presented problems of grave character. In 1948 the National Lutheran Council named Dr. Schiotz Executive Secretary for Younger Churches and Orphaned Missions and assigned him the herculean and uncharted task of finding direction for the postwar churches of the Third World. Although it was more than a decade since he had made his independent survey of the missions of the world, innumerable associations from that year now came to his aid. From this "crisis" assignment followed two years as director of World Missions for the Lutheran World

Federation, a post he surrendered when in 1954 he became the third president of his own church, the Evangelical Lutheran Church.

One of the immediate issues facing his presidency was ELC membership in the World Council of Churches. In 1948 the church convention had defeated a proposal for membership by a two-thirds majority vote. Two years after his election, in 1956, under Dr. Schiotz's deft and irenic leadership, the convention approved membership by a resounding majority. His vast ecumenical experience had equipped him for this hour. It has been said that President J. A. Aasgaard, his predecessor in office for more than 30 years, had led the church from its Norwegian roots into the American scene, and now Dr. Schiotz, in his 17 years, was to lead the church into the ecumenical world. To this work he brought a sound Lutheran confessionalism and a broad understanding of the *Una Sancta.*

Church mergers were the agenda when he took the helm, and by 1960 he had led his church into the new American Lutheran Church. Elected its first president, he now faced the arduous task of reorganizing structures and welding together four bodies which, though of common confession, brought with them long and separate traditions. His thorough understanding of the many churches and his basic pastoral heart brought him immediate acceptance and affection. When 11 years later he retired from office, he left a church which reflected the vigor of theological life, yet was relatively untouched by polarities and divisions, a church with a clear direction toward evangelical mission which he had given it.

The mergers of Lutheran bodies in the early '60s had brought the major part of Lutheranism in America into three large churches, the Lutheran Church-Missouri Synod, the Lutheran Church in America, and the American Lutheran Church. To bring these bodies into formal altar and pulpit fellowship, and into a working national council, became a pressing goal for the next years. Both these objectives were largely achieved during Schiotz's presidency, and not a little because of the patience, tenacity, and charity which he brought to the effort.

It was almost inevitable that the Lutheran World Federation would demand that he take his turn at leading this international body of 70 million Lutherans, and in Helsinki in 1963 he was elected its president, and served until its meeting in Evian in 1970.

The old question, "Does history shape the man, or does man shape history?" may well be asked about Fredrik Schiotz. Had he been born a century earlier, before the day of the ecumenical church, would the constellation of qualities that God had given him by birth and through his home have thrust him into leadership? Probably. Intelligence, dedication, industry, love of people, and sound judgment would have qualified him in any age.

For us who know him well, he is a friend. We trust him. There is nothing devious in his relationships. If he was a church politician, he was scarcely aware of it. He never consciously sought office. When summoned to a task, he accepted it as a servant. His personal habits are spartan. He has exemplified Kipling's words, "If you can talk with crowds and keep your virtue, or walk with kings—nor lose the common touch. . . ."

For more than 50 years, much of it in travel in this country and around the world, he has been sustained by the love and warmth of his wife, Dagny Aasen, who in her own right is a resourceful and remarkable woman.

Upon the urging of his many friends, Dr. Schiotz has written a short account of his life and work in this book.

Alvin N. Rogness

1

MY HERITAGE

THE FAMILY SURNAME *Schiotz* has been the occasion for confusion and questions all my life. People have generally assumed that it is of German origin. During the time I was in student work, I was a house guest of Dr. and Mrs. E. C. Stellhorn of Zion Lutheran Church on my first visit to Ann Arbor, Michigan. At the Sunday dinner, Mrs. Stellhorn, assuming I was of German ancestry but knowing that I was also serving Scandinavian constituency in the American Lutheran Conference, asked, "Tell me, are these Scandinavian people as nice as they seem to be?"

To this I replied, "I guess you have all kinds among them as well as among all other people." Before I left Ann Arbor, I gently broke the news to Mrs. Stellhorn that I was of Norwegian ancestry.

The Schiotz family (spelled Schiøtz in Europe) is Danish in

its origin. The earliest known member was a farmer who lived at Aarhus in Denmark (1615-1683). A grandson, Søren Schiøtz, studied law, was sent to Norway and became a judge in the city of Stavanger in 1769. (Norway was at this time under the Danish crown.) He remained in Norway and so today there are a considerable number of Schiøtzes in Norway as well as in Denmark. In the summer of 1936 I became posthumously acquainted with one of the ancestors, namely Søren Gabriel Schiøtz, for whom I have ever since felt a strong affinity.

This acquaintanceship was occasioned by the 1936 convention of the World Sunday School Association meeting in Oslo. While reading some of the convention printed matter, I noticed a story about a certain Søren Gabriel Schiøtz, who had helped to organize the first Sunday school in Norway. He had his home in the Stavanger area and had lived during the years 1804-1856. I decided to visit his grave in Stavanger. On the tombstone I found that he had also helped organize the Norwegian Mission Society, the Norwegian Israel Mission, and the Norwegian Bible Society. The grave marker concluded with a fascinating phrase: *han var fanternes ven,* "he was the friend of tramps."

My father, Jacob Schiotz, sailed for some years; but in 1887 he and his parents and sisters emigrated to the United States, settling in Chicago. There he followed the trade of a cabinetmaker.

Mother's father died while she was a small child. She was therefore entrusted to the care of relatives in Nordre Odalen in eastern Norway. When my mother was in her teens, my grandmother decided to emigrate to Chicago with her three daughters.

Father and Mother met in the young people's group at Bethlehem Lutheran Church in Chicago. At that time the congregation was served by Pastor J. N. Kildahl, later to become president of St. Olaf College and thereafter a professor at the United Lutheran Seminary in St. Paul. Kildahl had a rich ministry in Chicago. Under his shepherding both Father and Mother experienced a lively awareness of what it means to be a committed Christian. Hundreds of other youth were likewise helped. And so it came to be said that Pastor Kildahl had more spiritual sons and daughters than any other pastor in the church. Years later, in connection with Dr. Kildahl's funeral in Northfield, St. Olaf College held a memorial service. Dr. Donald Cowling, then president of Carleton College, said of Kildahl: "Some men build buildings, Kildahl built men."

Father and Mother were married by Pastor Kildahl. Not long thereafter he left Chicago to assume the presidency of St. Olaf, but the influence of Kildahl's ministry in Bethlehem congregation lingered for years. His name was a household word in our home throughout my childhood.

My first introduction to the name Kildahl occurred when I was four years old. At that age I had a tendency to stutter. One evening when I observed Father writing a letter, I asked what he was doing. To this he replied: "I am writing to the president of a school inviting him to speak at a mission festival in our church. When he comes, you must ask him whether you may attend his school when you grow up." This brief interchange was conducted in Norwegian, for that was the language used in our home.

In due time the mission festival took place. Dr. Kildahl was the guest speaker. After the meeting, refreshments were served in the church basement. When I spotted Kildahl in conversation with a group of people, I joined the group. Immediately, I blurted out in stuttered syllables, "Can (may) I go to your school when I grow up?" Kildahl, placing his hand on my head, inquired: "What are you saying, my boy?"

Father had come into the group just as my question was put. At once he interpreted my concern. I can still see the kindly eyes of Dr. Kildahl as he replied, "Indeed you may come to St. Olaf!" Those words were never forgotten.

Not long after this mission festival, the Rev. Hans Nesse, a missionary from China, visited a mission society in Bethlehem congregation. He was an overnight guest in our home. Conversations with him marked the beginning of an interest in China that grew and matured in later years.

Father always seemed robust and strong. But Mother appeared frail and prone to illness. In whispered conversation between her and Father, I learned that the family doctor had diagnosed a certain physical listlessness as the result of tuberculosis. He prescribed a daily portion of cod liver oil and as much rest as her family responsibilities would permit. The news seemed to drop a cloud over Mother's usual optimistic temperament.

When our pastor, the Rev. C. K. Solberg, learned of Mother's illness he called at our home. He listened to her story and shared her concern for the family. His reply assured Mother that the Lord was also concerned about the family. God willed her recovery that she might fulfill her ministry to the three children God had given her. He then invited Mother to kneel with him. There followed a moving prayer for healing. She rose from her knees with an inner assurance that health would be regained. And it was not long in coming.

Years later, when this experience was recalled, Mother told about a strange feeling of warmth that flowed through her body as Pastor Solberg prayed. No pastor dare lightly promise healing as categorically as did Pastor Solberg. But there may come times when you dare not do other. I have known such times in my own ministry as a pastor.

At five years of age, I contracted a serious cold. It settled in my throat. Infected glands brought about a swelling in the neck. Dr. Dahl, chief of staff at the Norwegian Deaconess Home and Hospital, diagnosed the trouble as tubercular glands. Surgery was prescribed. When my parents gave their hesitant consent, the operation was scheduled.

Father and Mother brought me to the hospital in the early evening of the day before the surgery. After a tearful farewell, the small hospital ward became oppressively quiet. Suddenly I was engulfed by loneliness. The struggle with this mood was interrupted by the entrance of a deaconess. She came directly to my bed. At once I recognized the friendly face of Sister Caroline who taught in our Sunday school. She visited with me for a while and then concluded with an evening prayer. The prayer made me feel at home. As Sister Caroline left the room, her farewell smile lifted my spirits. The loneliness had been dissipated and sleep took over.

The surgery was a four hour affair. Dr. Dahl pronounced it a success and told my parents that if no tubercular infection should break out within the next seven years, he would know that the surgery had been done in time.

One episode stands out from that first year in school where I was enrolled at the age of six. One day the teacher announced that we would begin rehearsing for a program to be given for a school festival. Our class contribution was to be a singing event. The number to be sung was announced. Each child was asked to bury his face in folded arms on the desk. The teacher would visit each desk, bend her head to listen to the quiet singing of the child. The testing began. When the teacher had completed her monitoring, she announced the results. It seemed to me that almost the entire class had been selected. I and two or three others were not among the elect.

The disappointment was a first step in learning one of my limitations. Later, the teacher's judgment was confirmed by my father's kidding. If I tried singing in the house, Father remarked: "Did someone pinch the cat's tail again?" After confirmation studies, I tried out for the church choir in a small congregation in northern Wisconsin. The organist's facial expression gave me my verdict.

Father had developed a restlessness about continued city living. The recollection of his boyhood years on a large farm near Sandness, Norway, asserted itself. Father and Mother were both ready to listen when a real estate agent called. He represented a sawmill-lumber firm at Hawkins in northern Wisconsin. The fact that the lumber firm was Scandinavian owned made it that much more appealing. A contract was signed for the purchase of 40 acres of land. Two other Chicago families had preceded us to Hawkins. They became a welcoming committee for us.

The family economy did not permit us to move onto the 40-acre plot of land that had been bought. There were no buildings on the acreage and trees would have to be felled, and stumps pulled before cultivation and planting could begin. Actually, such a task is a lifetime endeavor. But father's yearnings were nourished with anticipation. He secured a job as a lumber grader and we settled down in Hawkins, a small, friendly village. For Mother and Father the presence of a Norwegian Lutheran congregation with a resident pastor gave it an "A" rating.

It was in Hawkins that we learned to fish and to play baseball. Fishing began with a bent pin and much frustration; but when fishhooks were obtained, it became sheer recreation.

The love for baseball that began in those years has remained throughout life. It also introduced me to the restrictive provision of a day of rest. Our closest neighbor was a devout Methodist family. The youngest son was a daily companion of ours. But his parents would not allow him to play baseball on Sunday. Father and Mother required Sunday school and church attendance. But after that Sunday was open for any wholesome activity. I had not been given a formal theological interpretation of Luther's evangelical teaching about Sunday observance. However, I sensed there was a difference in an evangelical interpretation and a legalistic understanding. This recognition of the Christian freedom wherein my parents lived evoked a deep feeling of gratitude for them.

We had not been in Hawkins long before the Lutheran congregation drafted my father to serve as Sunday school superintendent. This became a mutually satisfying experience until we were on the threshold of Christmas. A small Methodist congregation had no church home of its own. The Lutheran church was placed at their disposal for a Sunday evening parish school and worship service. It was suggested that the two Sunday schools should put on a joint Christmas program. Father welcomed the idea and everything went well until the first joint rehearsal. In the Methodist program of recitations several made Santa Claus the center of attention. In the consultation that followed the rehearsal, Father said that he understood Christmas to be a day when Christ was to be honored. He suggested that the Santa Claus pieces be dropped. The suggestion was rejected.

This bit of theological disagreement was referred to the Lutheran pastor. He approved of the joint Christmas program as it was. Father's convictions could not accept the pastor's ruling. He therefore submitted his resignation as Sunday school superintendent. For several weeks thereafter some boys in town called me "Santa Claus."

When the Christmas program was over and it was time to reconvene the Sunday school, there was no leadership for it. The pastor came to Father to ask him to take up the task anew. To this request Father said *yes*. That thrilled me. He didn't sulk. His witness had been made by his protest. That done, he was ready to carry on so that the children might be nurtured in the faith.

The pastor in Hawkins had several other congregations to serve. That meant that Sunday morning services were conducted about every third Sunday in Hawkins. The small Methodist congregation held worship services on Sunday evenings whenever a pastor could come in from a neighboring congregation to conduct them. If a Methodist service coincided with a Sunday when there was no Lutheran worship, Father would attend. In the fall of our second year in Hawkins, I accompanied my father to a Methodist service. Mother remained at home to care for two younger brothers.

The recollection of that evening has remained with me through the years. A Pastor Oliver was the preacher. His sermon portrayed a Christ whose love for mankind drove him to offer his life on Calvary's cross for the sin of all mankind. As I sat beside my father and listened, it was as though a voice spoke: "He did this for you." Quietly my mind affirmed that I was included in this outreach of love. The thought then arose: "What can I do in appreciation?" For my child's mind of nine years, it seemed right that I should offer to serve as a pastor or as an overseas missionary. The choice was made. There followed an inner satisfaction accompanied by the feeling that I had answered a call from the Man of Galilee.

There were no histrionics in Pastor Oliver's preaching that evening. But his speaking exuded confidence in the Lord he was proclaiming. For others who were worshiping, the service may have seemed just another service. For me it was an event.

As I walked beside my father on the way home, I confided in him what had transpired. He asked whether I would be willing to tell Mother what I had shared with him. This seemed right, and I agreed to do it.

When we reached home, Father suggested to Mother that the three of us sit down at the kitchen table. He then invited me to repeat what I had told him. When I concluded, Father led in an evening prayer wherein he asked that God would keep me faithful and bless me in my decision. Thereafter, very little was said in the family about what had happened. There was only one discernible difference: it was generally understood that the family expected me to go on to college when that time came.

The congregation at Hawkins was a member of the United Norwegian Lutheran Church. In this church it was the custom for the president of a circuit (conference) to conduct an occasional visitation in each congregation. During a visitation the circuit president would ask the assembled congregation about its faith, the congregation's activities, and the moral life of its members.

The Rev. J. E. Nord of Rice Lake, Wisconsin, wearer of a long patriarchal beard, was circuit president at that time. He visited Hawkins in the early fall of 1911. The meeting moved along well until he asked the question, "Do any members of the congregation dance?" A long pause set in. Then Mr. C. K. Ellingson, majority owner of the sawmill and lumber company, replied, "No, they do not."

Many members of the congregation belonged to the Norwegian Lodge, and the lodge sponsored Saturday evening dances from time to time. It was a well-known community fact that church members participated in these dances. Father's compelling sense of honesty led him to say, "Yes, some do." President Nord did not know what to write in his record book and so looked inquiringly at the pastor. But Mr. Ellingson was not to be brooked by any appeal. In a stentorian voice he intruded with the words, "Absolutely no." Pastor Nord then proceeded to other matters.

A few weeks after the circuit president's visit, a regular congregational meeting was held. In an appropriate agenda spot, Father called for the floor. He directed a question to Mr. Ellingson, "Why did you in the recent meeting with Pastor Nord answer his question about dancing in the negative? It is a well-known fact that there are members in the congregation who do dance?" This question so infuriated Mr. Ellingson that he rose in the meeting and fired my father.

One may well question the merit of the type of inquiry made by President Nord. In that day it was not unusual. Dancing was simply labeled as sin. But the primary question in Father's exchange with Mr. Ellingson was a fact of honesty. Father hated all forms of sham and hypocrisy. It was good to grow up in a family where there was a lively respect for honesty.

This wholesome attitude was undergirded by the good relationship that existed between Father and Mother. There was no question but what Father was head of the household; nevertheless, Mother was in charge of the finances. Father was a strict disciplinarian, but discipline was tempered by a concern for what was fair and just. In the mornings Mother sent us off to school after a brief breakfast devotional. In the evening, the moment dinner was over, either I or my brother brought Father the Bible, his pipe, and tobacco. A chapter from the Bible, Father's prayer and the singing of a familiar hymn concluded the dinner vespers. Thereafter Father turned to his pipe.

Father's discharge from work at the congregational meeting in Hawkins brought an end to his dream of developing the 40-acre tract of land he contracted for while we were still in Chicago. The Ellingson Lumber Company was practically the sole employer in town. It was therefore necessary to look elsewhere for employment. The most likely place seemed to be Ladysmith, the county seat, no more than 20 miles west on the Soo Line Railway. The decision to go there to seek work was placed before God in prayer. His leading and direction was invoked.

The Soo Line train to Ladysmith came through Hawkins between five and six o'clock in the morning. Father was on his way the Monday after he had collected his last paycheck. On the train he met a man named Walter Morgan who was also on his way to Ladysmith. He told Father that he was going to move his family to Ladysmith, but first he had to build a house. When he learned that Father was a carpenter, he hired him at once. When Father returned the next weekend, he and Mother thanked God for his providence. Plans were then made to move as soon as Father could find a place for the family to live.

Housing was scarce in Ladysmith that fall. Father had to settle for a vacated store building. But in the spring a new four-room house became available on the south side. It was bought on a contract with monthly amortization payments. The purchase price was $800. This house remained our home until after the death of my father.

There were two Lutheran congregations in Ladysmith: one belonging to the Iowa Synod and the second one a member of the United Norwegian Lutheran Church. St. Paul's of the Iowa Synod used only German for its parish activities. The Norwegian congregation was without a pastor and no services were conducted. In this situation, we attended the Methodist church the first Sunday after our arrival in Ladysmith. My sister, I, and one brother were entered in the Methodist Sunday school. My sister and I also participated in the Epworth League.

It was not long before a committee from the Methodist church called at our home. We were given a warm invitation to join the congregation. Father responded with appreciation for the invitation. He then explained that we were Lutherans, but that our congregation would not have a pastor until spring. Meanwhile, we would like to continue in the Methodist congregation as guests. He concluded by thanking them for the warm hospitality the congregation had shown us. Thus, very early in life I was exposed to a point of view that honored the Lutheran confessional stance but refused to ignore Christians in other households of faith. This was my first lesson in ecumenicity.

When the Morgan house was completed, Father sought work with the Flambeau River Lumber Company. Once again, he became a lumber grader. Little did we realize that this job would in a few years rob Father of his health. Father was strong and healthy, but he was smaller in stature than I. The lumber, cut from logs that had been floated down the Flambeau River, was green and heavy with water. Handling this lumber 10 hours each day and six days per week, exacted a heavy toll.

Father encouraged participation in the sports that were available to us. Baseball, swimming, skating, and skiing claimed prior attention during grade school years. Most of the boys with whom I played went swimming without parental permission. For me to do this seemed like the violation of a confidence that had been posited in me by my parents. I therefore asked Father for permission. He granted it at once but with the stipulation that I should not go beyond my depth until I had learned to swim and he had had an opportunity to inspect. The happy day arrived when I could announce that I had learned to swim and would like his approval for swimming to a pier in the river from where the diving was done. Father plied me with many questions. Satisfied, he gave his consent to my request without conducting an inspection. The mutuality of trust that this transaction called forth was as satisfying as the swimming itself.

When the Rev. John Ritland, who graduated from Luther Seminary in St. Paul in May 1912, arrived to shepherd the Ladysmith congregation and three others, we withdrew from activity at the Methodist church. We had no church building of our own, but were welcome tenants of St. Paul's Lutheran Church. For Sunday school we used the woodworking shop of a faithful bachelor member.

It was not long before enthusiasm was ignited for the acquisition of our own church property. But resources were very limited, and loans from the synod were unavailable. The building program proceeded as it did in so many home mission congregations of that day: first a basement was built and taken into use. Later a superstructure was erected but with no interior finish. In the center, slightly to one side, was a large box stove set in a sandpit. In due time the interior of the church was finished. Each stage of work saw some members donating labor. The completed church was no cathedral, but it took a decade to finish it. For me it became the primary spiritual home of childhood and teen years.

Under Pastor Ritland, Father was drafted to serve as superintendent of the Sunday school. He was also asked to serve as the congregation's precentor. If the congregation entertained a circuit convention, a visiting pastor might be entertained in our home. Such a time provided me with a stimulating experience in listening to Father and the pastor discuss the Bible and its meanings. In those listening periods, theological understanding began to emerge.

A Luther League was organized under Pastor Ritland. In the first years anyone interested attended Luther League. It seemed more like a meeting of adults than youth. But youth were drafted to participate in programs with readings and declamations. It became a wholesome fellowship of people of all ages—a family such as a congregation is intended to be. Some years later, Luther League meetings were reserved for youth only. Some gains were made but it is questionable whether the gains outweighed the losses.

One year a considerable discussion developed over whether we should continue to serve refreshments after League meetings. I supported the discontinuance of post-League snacks and this became the decision. The most ardent supporter in favor of continuing refreshments were some brothers who lived on a farm. Later, I realized I had been wrong in my position. Those from the country had walked into town a considerable distance and were actually hungry. How important it is to maintain perspective: know your neighbor's point of view.

A Circuit Luther League organization was brought into being. Annual conventions were held. In 1917, when the 400th anniversary of the Reformation was sponsored, the program committee assigned to me the responsibility of giving a talk on *Luther at the Wartburg.* The preparation of the talk provided new acquaintance with the life of Martin Luther. But the delivery of the talk occasioned much concern and nervousness. The convention was at Rice Lake. After the Sunday meal, I took a long walk pondering my afternoon's assignment. As I returned to the church, while I was yet several blocks away, I could hear the choir rehearsing. Their anthem was the hymn "Come Ye Disconsolate." Those strains from the choir became like balm for my soul and settled my mind. Nervousness all but disappeared. I was ready for the afternoon.

That experience in Rice Lake long ago left such a strong impression that it has remained with me through the years. Two years ago when my wife and I drove through Rice Lake, we stopped, parked the car, and reminisced. The old church has been replaced, but my walk and reflection retraced the terrain of that Sunday in the summer of 1917.

Father had worked for the Flambeau River Lumber Company about three years when his health failed. Shortness of breath had afflicted him for several months. Dr. Lundmark, our respected family physician, diagnosed the illness as "heart trouble." Very soberly the doctor announced that if health were to be regained, he would have to leave the heavy work in the lumber yard. But what does a man with family responsibilities (four children) do in such a situation? There was then neither workmen's compensation, pension plans, nor public assistance. The family prayed for a way out. God's answer seemed to come in an opportunity for Father to become a custodian for the south side school.

The custodianship provided a way whereby the family could help with a good deal of the work. But our help was not enough to stay Father's deteriorating health. After about 18 months, he had to resign. Soon after he became bedridden. He was a bed patient at home for a year, pains in the abdominal area becoming increasingly severe. The last several months the pain became so intense that they brought on dark moments of doubt.

To Father it was now clear that the end was not too far away. One Sunday afternoon he called us all together. He asked each of us children successively, beginning with my sister who was the oldest, to kneel at his bedside. Then, like Jacob of old, he placed his hand on our heads, spoke a brief prayer and invoked God's blessing. He then turned to me as the oldest son and charged me with responsibility for my younger brother, then five years old.

I had continued to hope for a miraculous recovery for Father. Could there not be a healing for him such as the one Mother experienced? To that end I vowed that I would remain awake all night in a prayer vigil asking God to grant healing. My vigil was interrupted by my falling asleep. When I awoke, guilt weighed heavily because of my failure to remain alert. I took refuge in the certainty of God's love and in the inner assurance that God who knows all things knew also that my intent was honorable.

After this experience, I did some more reflection on the place of prayer and its relation to God's answer. As my mind visualized Christ praying in the Garden of Gethsemane, I became aware that God does not always answer prayer according to our prescription. The *no* given to our Lord will also have to be the answer given to his followers from time to time. I was then ready to accept the likelihood that Father would not recover.

For a few weeks after this he seemed to be more alert than he had been for some time. The pain abated. And then when we all thought it safe to seek rest, Mother included, he slept away on the night of September 26, 1916, five days short of his 51st birthday.

The funeral service conducted by our pastor, the presence of friends and relatives from Illinois and Indiana cushioned the hurt and the sense of loss. In fact, there was a taste of Easter present and the sublimated joy which it confers.

The relatives had left some gifts of money with Mother. No money had been paid to our family physician, Dr. Lundmark. He had faithfully made a number of house calls during Father's long illness, and Mother felt distressed that there had been no payments. She took the money received from relatives and called at Dr. Lundmark's office. She announced that she wanted to make a payment on account. Dr. Lundmark, ever the friendly and brusque person that he was, replied, "You don't have any money, Mrs. Schiotz!"

Mother announced that she had received some gifts from relatives. Quickly he replied, "And I should take those gifts from you? No!" How many doctors and lawyers are there now who have ministered to community needs without any ostentation?

The absence of a paycheck after Father's resignation as school janitor seemed to place an economic barrier to the future. Mother must have worried some; but there was no visible evidence of it. She remained calm and hopeful. She cast her burdens upon the Lord. And he did not bring her to shame in the confidence she posited in him. Mother did some laundry work. Before long an opportunity opened up for my sister to work as cashier in one of the two largest stores in town. She was still a student in the eighth grade, but she gave up further opportunity to study and worked full time. Her $8 per week became the family's primary support base for several months.

When Father died I had just entered the eighth grade. Mother and my sister opposed my dropping out of school. But I sought some part-time work. I secured a job in a local hardware store. Arrangements were made to work from 7 to 8:30 each morning. The school superintendent allowed me to leave school early in the afternoon so that work at the store could begin again between 2:30 and 3 o'clock and on to 6:30, the store's closing hour. Saturdays the work period was from 7 A.M. to 9 P.M. For this I was paid $3 per week. Both my sister and I turned our money over to Mother who managed the finances.

The eighth grade school year was the beginning of acquaintance with two great teachers—who contributed very much to my life. Many elementary and high school teachers are remembered, with gratitude, but two remain in a class by themselves: Gertrude Musgrove and Edwin M. Dahlberg.

Miss Musgrove was a diminutive woman, probably no more than four feet, six inches in height. She was from Massachusetts, a direct descendant of the child born aboard the Mayflower. Despite Miss Musgrove's size, she was an excellent disciplinarian.

This she accomplished quietly, almost entirely through the approval or disapproval reflected by her eyes. Her presence was that of a cultured lady. My sister had been in her class when she quit school to go to work. She was therefore well acquainted with our family situation.

Miss Musgrove became my teacher the fall Father died. A couple of weeks after the funeral she called me aside for some conversation. She said that because of our family's circumstances it would be desirable that I move forward in school as rapidly as possible. Then she added that she had discussed with the superintendent the possibility of my being transferred at once to the first year in high school. He had approved this providing that she would tutor me in algebra so that I might be abreast of the class that I would join. Thereafter, for several Saturdays, I received private instruction in her home.

The full implications of Miss Musgrove's generosity registered more fully 10 years later when I was a high school teacher myself. I wrote her a letter of appreciation with some news about what had happened during the intervening years. Under date of October 26, 1926, I received a three-page letter in reply wherein she observed, ". . . I am sure a Divine Helper has upheld you. . . ."

Mr. Dahlberg was our high school principal and science teacher. He taught only juniors and seniors and so I might have missed contact with him during the first two years of high school except for the fact that he coached those who went out for oratory. Under Mr. Dahlberg, the practice was intensive. Since I was working in the afternoon, he met me in the high school auditorium in the evenings. He would move from place to place in the auditorium to test the projection of my voice. He insisted on clipped pronunciation. He wanted to hear every word without my ever resorting to shouting. It was drill, drill, and more drilling. This coach made my style of speaking. Whenever people have told me that they find it easy to hear me in public address, I always say, "This is something I owe to my high school coach."

In my senior year I auditioned to represent our high school in oratory. Mr. Dahlberg encouraged me to write my own oration although this was not usually done. When I accepted this proposal, it followed that I must have a topic. He suggested that I write something on the health hazards of cigarette smoking. He called attention to some reports from the Ford Foundation at Dearborn, Michigan, that brought a strong indictment against cigarettes. The findings were not much different than those reported in recent years by the U.S. Surgeon General's office. And so the topic was selected and the title for the oration became "The Little White Slaver."

In the Ladysmith contest April 25, 1919, I won the right to represent our high school. May 2 I won the district contest in Colby, and the regional was won at Eau Claire May 9.

I returned from the Eau Claire trip on a train that got into Ladysmith about 5 o'clock in the morning. When Mother met me at the door, I could see that she was happy about the result. But there was no word of congratulation. Her first word was, "Fredrik, you must not be proud." Many pedagogs would say that this was the wrong thing to say in such a homecoming. But I knew Mother well enough so that I derived encouragement from her intent.

The next week the school board announced that it could not afford to send Mr. Dahlberg, my coach, to accompany me to the state contest at Madison. Mr. Dahlberg was disappointed, but I more so. The zest for the trip and the combat had left me.

En route to Madison, I changed trains early in the morning at Waukesha. Then my pocket was either picked or my travel money was lost. A friendly brakeman on the Madison train loaned me money for what remained of the journey.

My arrival in Madison coincided with a city "welcome home" to the *Rainbow Division* of Wisconsin combat boys. Free cigarette packages were given as a part of the welcome ceremony. And in the afternoon I was to speak on the university campus about "The Little White Slaver." I do not have the records of that contest, but it is my recollection that I placed fourth or fifth out of 10 contestants.

The writing of the oration spurred Mr. Dahlberg to encourage me to do some more writing. I participated in a Wisconsin Civil Service Commission contest and won a certificate for our high school. I also submitted a slogan with a paragraph essay for a contest sponsored by a trade journal titled "Philadelphia Made Hardware." I won the first prize, $30 in War Savings Stamps. The award arrived in time to be used for the purchase of my high school commencement suit.

The associations with Mr. Dahlberg in school activities fostered a friendship. He lived in a house on the edge of town with the Flambeau River 20 feet below. In the summer after commencement, occasional evenings and frequent Sunday afternoons were spent with Dahlberg and his wife Mary.

The Flambeau was a series of rapids and falls between Park Falls and Ladysmith. This stretch of water, sometimes tumbling in a foam of white water, and at other places rolling with haste through rapids, and then for a stretch relaxing in leisurely flow, traversed a wilderness of trees. It was a canoer's paradise.

To the fellowship in speech work that bound Dahlberg and me in friendship there was now added a love of the river and the forest it nurtured. One evening he read to me Byron E. Veatch's five and one-half page soliloquy about the Flambeau River which he titled *My River*. It is hauntingly beautiful. When Dahlberg had completed the reading, we agreed that Mr. Veatch had identified many of our thoughts and feelings. It was "our river," but there was no resentment in knowing that Mr. Veatch regarded the Flambeau as "My River."

2

NEW INSIGHTS

AFTER HIGH SCHOOL THERE WAS an interesting year of work in a hardware store, and then enrollment at St. Olaf College in Northfield, Minnesota. College was followed by two years of teaching in the high school of my home town of Ladysmith, Wisconsin. Thereafter came three years of study at Luther Theological Seminary in St. Paul, interrupted after the first year by nine months serving as a traveling secretary for the Student Volunteer Movement for Foreign Missions.

During my teenage years there were some legalisms which, at the time, seemed like a part of the Christian faith. Dancing, use of alcoholic beverages, and public discussion of sex were taboo. This was true in my home community and also on the St. Olaf College campus. In fact, during college days I became acquainted with a new legalism called "unionism." This term referred to joint worship services or fellowship with congregations that belonged to churches with whom there was no formal pulpit and altar fellowship.

Today we may smile at such opinions. In doing so, we may overlook the fact that almost all religions develop some forms of legalism that seem irrational. I recall that many years later, while I was serving the Lutheran World Federation I conducted some discussions with the government of Israel in the interest of securing their release of certain mission properties that they had appropriated. When the discussions had been completed, the government man with whom I had been dealing suggested that we make a courtesy call on the Chief Rabbi in Jeruslem. I answered yes at once.

The appointment was arranged for noon on the next Sabbath day, after the rabbi would have returned from his responsibilities at the synagogue. When we arrived at the rabbi's home, my goveernment companion knocked on the door. He did it a second time but there was no response. Meanwhile, during my companion's knocking I spotted an electric bell button. I was about to press the button when my friend pushed my hand aside, and exclaimed, "No! No! It is the Sabbath!"

The beginning of my change from a legalistic life-style to practicing the freedom of the gospel began during college days. There was no sudden thrusting aside of the religious and cultural traditions in which I had grown up. But my mind began to ask questions of myself. Then came a release through a biblical insight that has throughout life seemed like a very precious personal possession. In fact, this truth has always remained to assist with direction in recognizing God's will in my decisions. But before I turn to that let me trace some of the elements that were preparatory along the way.

My interest in foreign missions was sharpened through the associations in the mission society at St. Olaf. Dagny, my wife, whose acquaintance I made in my sophomore year, was also interested in missionary work as a life calling. This led us to identify with the Student Volunteer Movement for Foreign Missions. In doing this we signed a declaration card wherein we stated: "I purpose, God permitting, to become a foreign missionary." The focus of our commitment was China. Shortly after this the state Student Volunteer Movement (SVM) convention met on our campus. I was elected president. This responsibility led to national contacts while representing Minnesota on the SVM National Council.

Every four years the national SVM sponsored an American-Canadian convention. During the Christmas-New Year week of 1923-24 the convention met at Indianapolis. More than 6100 people, representing 841 institutions, were present. Of these, 4900 were students. And not a few were black students.

Indianapolis introduced me to Christian leaders of international repute: John R. Mott, Robert E. Speer, Robert Wilder, Henry P. Van Dusen, G. A. Studdert-Kennedy, J. E. K. Aggrey, a great name in Africa of that day, and many others. What a satisfaction it was to hear Bible-centered messages that nurtured mind and heart, with sensitive application to issues of daily life, here and abroad. Personal commitment to Christ and God's will was always to the fore.

In the spring of 1923 the St. Olaf student senate received an invitation to send representatives to an inter-Lutheran convention at Augustana College, Rock Island, Illinois. The objective was to organize a Lutheran Student Association that would serve students of all Lutheran Synods. The student senate thought the time inopportune; final exams seemed too close at hand, and therefore they voted not to be represented.

President L. W. Boe was deeply disappointed in the student decision. A day or two after he received the student senate decision, I met him on the steps of the Old Main. In an imperative tone of voice, he barked out, "Schiotz, you go to Rock Island." And he handed me an envelope with information about the convention and told me to go to the treasurer's office for the necessary travel money.

At Rock Island I was elected president of this newly constituted association. The responsibilities that followed brought me into contact with leaders in each of the Lutheran churches except the Lutheran Church-Missouri Synod. I found none who subscribed to the "doctrinal liberalism" that so many attributed to the United Lutheran Church in America. But very few ULCA leaders approved of the legalism that bothered many Scandinavian Lutherans.

After Rock Island I received a letter from Dr. O. A. Tingelstad, secretary of the Board of Trustees of Luther College at Decorah, Iowa. He criticized me severely for accepting the LSAA presidency. He declared me guilty of "unionism" and of violating the articles of union that brought three Norwegian Lutheran bodies together in 1917. Because of this criticism he asked me to share the letter with President Boe. Dr. Boe read the letter, smiled, and cautioned against allowing such criticism to disturb me.

A few years later (after my first year at Luther Seminary), I was invited by the SVM to become a part of their traveling secretarial staff during the next school year. The invitation arrived while I was doing summer work for the Rev. L. N. Field of Williston, North Dakota. We talked about it and he suggested that it provided an opportunity for missionary service and some valuable experience. In further prayer and reflection I became convinced that acceptance was God's will for me.

As I traveled east enroute to New York and the offices of the SVM, I stopped off in the Twin Cities. I felt that courtesy required that I notify the officers of Luther Seminary that I would be gone for a year. I sought an appointment with Dr. O. E. Brandt, the vice-president of the seminary. When I announced that I had accepted the SVM invitation, he replied, "You must not do this." He then volunteered to take the responsibility if I would reject the commitment that I had made. To this I answered that no man can assume responsibility for another person's decisions. But he continued to insist that I must change my decision. Finally, he said, "You better talk to President Böckman." (The president had been in Norway on a year's leave of absence and I did not know that he was back.)

I had never met President Böckman, but I had heard much about him. He was reputed to be an able New Testament scholar and a man of sterling Christian character. I therefore went to his office with anticipation. Courteously, he inquired in Norwegian, "What is on your mind?" I told him my story. He responded, "If you ask my opinion, I don't think you should travel for the SVM this coming school year; but I will not deny that it might be God's will for you."

After a few more exchanges in conversation, he arose. As he did this, he put his hand on my shoulder and said, "If you remain convinced that it is God's will that you stay away from the seminary this year, then God bless you in your mission." In that moment the easy use of the scare word "unionism" lost its threat for me. And I would have traveled across the world to get back to Luther Seminary a year later.

When I returned to the seminary a year later, the student body was thrust into a debate on the "sin of unionism." An invitation was received from the students at the Evangelical Lutheran Seminary at Columbus, Ohio, to participate in an inter-synodical Lutheran seminary convention. A motion was offered from the floor at a regular student body meeting to accept the invitation and to authorize the appointment of delegates. Immediately a lively discussion ensued. There was not time to complete it, and so further consideration was deferred until after lunch.

When the business meeting reconvened, one of the students raised a question about unionism. Since our church did not have fellowship with the other churches whose seminaries would be represented, would we not be ignoring the union stipulations of

1917? (The reference was to the union of the Norwegian Synod, the United Norwegian Evangelical Lutheran Church, and the Hauge Synod.) That brought forth strong protest from those who favored the proposal. Tempers rose and it seemed best to table the motion for another day. When the vote came, the proposal to participate in the Columbus convention carried by a small margin.

Social dancing was not permitted by congregations in the former Evangelical Lutheran Church. The five senior colleges of the church forbade dancing. At St. Olaf I recall several students who were brought before the student senate, charged with a breach of college regulations regarding dancing. The fact that it had been done off campus did not extenuate the charge.

Later, when I was a high school teacher, I advised the superintendent that I would be glad to help in any type of extra curricular activity. But I drew the line on chaperoning high school dances.

This arbitrary position on social dancing was supported by the general assumption that it would lead to violation of the Sixth Commandment. And this, of course, was true of many public dances. Boys went with the intent of "warming up" a girl for later sexual intercourse.

My change in outlook resulted during several quarters of study at the University of Chicago. In the course of preparing a class paper I found a book in the library that reported a study of youth sponsored recreation in the churches of Morris, Illinois. The author had spent considerable time interviewing young people. In fact, he had spent time with them in the ice cream parlors of the city. This led to acquaintance, trust, and acceptance. He was one of them in the conversation huddles.

He learned that all the mainline Protestant churches in Morris allowed social dancing as part of the recreation in youth work. But the Lutheran congregation did not. I knew immediately that it was an ELC congregation, and its emphasis was in keeping with the position of the church in all its congregations.

The writer of the book went beyond this initial probing. He checked the city's record on unmarried mothers. This information obtained, he investigated church affiliations. There were more unmarried mothers among the girls from the Lutheran congregation than from any of the other Protestant churches.

This factual data stopped me cold. Had I been wrong all along in my attitude toward the dance? Some careful reflection on my presuppositions (and those of the church) began. Through renewed Bible study and evaluation of the psychological factors in temptation new light dawned.

Strong prohibitions make the thing that is prohibited much more desirable. The church, legitimately concerned about chastity, was defeating its own purpose. The friendly coming together of youth in social dancing could actually contribute to building up wholesome and positive relations. Today none of our senior colleges forbid dancing as a part of the social program on the campus.

While I was in student work for the American Lutheran Conference, I received an invitation to address the national Luther League convention of the Augustana Synod scheduled to meet at Rockford, Illinois, in February of 1941. I was asked to give a Valentine's Day address using Psalm 127:1 as my theme: "Unless the Lord builds the house, their labor is in vain who build it" (KJV).

The evening before I was to travel to Rockford, I had been meeting with the Lutheran student group at the University of Wisconsin. After the meeting I went to my hotel room in Madison. The outline for my address at Rockford was ready, but I was not satisfied with it. The source of my dissatisfaction was the question of honesty. Should I allow the romantic generalities that are identified with Valentine's Day be the substance of my address? At that time public discussion of the sexual relationships in marriage was almost unknown in church circles. But I knew it was on the mind of all healthy teenagers. Should I use the beautiful first verse in Psalm 127 to thrust me into the heart of biblical realism regarding the love relationship in the home they expected to have? I decided that it had to be this—despite the possibility of jolting the sensitivities of many people.

I was not altogether unprepared to do this. I had prepared for such an eventuality by taking a correspondence course with Dr. Paul Popenoe's Los Angeles-based American Institute for Family Relationships. This institute, organized in 1930, was probably the first of its kind offering scientific information with wholesome psychological insights.

In my address I stressed the positive: the Creator had purpose in making us as we are, male and female. Genesis records God's judgment: "It is not good that man should be alone" (2:18a). The companionship is to be mutually enriching, the paramount human relationship in life: "Therefore a man leaves his father and mother and cleaves to his wife, and they become one flesh" (2:24). In this statement there is no room for thinking of the physical relationship in marriage as something unclean; to the contrary, it is regarded as holy and good.

Adam and Eve were told to "Be fruitful and multiply and fill the earth and subdue it" (1:28b). From this statement many conclude that birth control should not be used by Christians. But the command to "multiply and fill the earth" was something different in the dawn of history than it is now when there is overpopulation and starvation in many parts of the world. While there is good reason to exercise the stewardship of family planning, this is no justification to say, "We will not have children."

After the address the expressions of gratitude were much more than the perfunctory appreciation statements that follow a talk that has been well received. A new atmosphere pervaded the church where the convention sessions met. It was as though people were saying, "Now we need no longer talk about sex in dark corners with hushed voices. It is a gift of God to be used according to his gracious will."

News about the Rockford address spread not only in the Augustana Synod, but also in the ELC and in the ULCA. Dr. T. F. Gullixson, president of Luther Seminary, invited me to address the ELC pastors at the annual seminary convocation. He suggested that I speak on premarital counseling. I asked Dr. Gullixson, "Am I free to speak as I think I should in discussing this issue?" He hesitated before giving his answer. Then suddenly a smile spread across his face and he replied, "Say whatever you think should be said."

When the day came for the address, the small seminary chapel was packed. I spoke simply but honestly about what is required in the pastor's attitude if he is to be helpful to people that seek counsel regarding sex and family life.

Not long after this I was invited by the Sunday school teachers in the St. Paul Conference of ELC congregations to give a series of lectures, one each week over a span of six weeks. The lectures were to be a Christian treatment of the sexual life.

The United Lutheran Church in America (ULCA) sponsored the publication of a journal titled *The Lutheran Church Quarterly*. The editor had heard about my lecture to the Luther Seminary convocation for pastors. He asked for permission to publish it in their *Quarterly*. This was granted and it appeared in the issue for October 1945.

I now return to what I promised in the first part of this chapter—the story of my own inner release from a life-style that was bound by custom and man-made rules. It became clear to me that whatever the legalism may be, it is essentially a form of idolatry. We embrace some principle that we regard as good. It is lifted up before others and carefully safeguarded by rules and regulations. This appears to make the good life a simple experience. But the simplicity disappears under the burden of man-made law.

My awareness of this and the consequent release to live under the gospel broke in upon my mind through two biblical readings. The first one is found in Genesis 22. The second is from Jesus' words in Luke 14:26-27, 33.

Genesis 22 presents the story of Abraham and God's command that he sacrifice his son, Isaac. It was clear that Abraham had come to love his son to the degree that all of life centered in him. God saw that this possessive love threatened the welfare of both father and son. The Mount Moriah trip taught Abraham "to let go." Thereafter his possessiveness ceased and he could love Isaac with fatherly maturity. Søren Kierkegaard has called Abraham's experience "eternity's double movement." This is to say that all of us will have some possessive loves. Whenever we face up to this and are consciously ready to let go, God may return our "Isaac" to us. That's why it may be called a double movement—to and from Mount Moriah. But because temptations will continue to afflict us, coming back in ever new forms, Kierkegaard called it "eternity's" movement.

The words of Jesus in Luke 14 deal with the same truth that is articulated in Genesis 22. The only difference is that Jesus' words are more inclusive. He puts his finger on three values that can easily become an "Isaac" for us: relatives and human relationships, self, and possessions. He announces that unless a person is willing to let go of these loves (that is, to hold them in an open hand), "he cannot be my disciple."

The Lord is not saying here that he does not want you. He is declaring that you cannot be a disciple, you cannot learn of him. The idolatries of life can block the possibility of deriving meaning and blessing from the truths (mysteries) of the kingdom.

Two illustrations, one a negative one and then a positive action, may be helpful. During the economic depression that followed the stock market crash of 1929, hundreds of thousands of people lost a life's savings. I recall a man who was a very active member in one of our Lutheran congregations. He had made a considerable investment in the stock market.

After the crash he used his noon hour to make daily visits to his broker for news about the market. In these visits he was hoping to get news that the market was about to make a sustained comeback. But it didn't happen. With each day's report the outlook become more bleak. After many weeks there came a day when he felt that a decision had to be made. In the evening he returned home and had dinner with his family. The dinner concluded, he did what was usual. He led the family in a tableside vesper service. Thereafter he went down in the basement and hung himself.

There is nothing wrong in owning stocks or properties. But when stocks or other possessions own us, we are no longer free people.

The second illustration is a glorious commentary on the freedom in Christ. I was visiting in Rajahmundry, India. The missionary had asked me to speak to a group of students. These young people normally gathered in the city YMCA once a week during the noon hour. While I was speaking two young men came in late and had to stand up in the back of the room. They gave the appearance of being good friends. This impression was strengthened when I had an opportunity to visit with them after the meeting. One of them was called Mr. Paul and the other was designated Mr. John.

In walking away from the YMCA building, I called the missionary's attention to these two young men. He knew them well and told me that Mr. John was of the outcaste group in Hindu society; but he had been a Christian many years. Mr. Paul was a Brahmin, the top caste among hundreds in the Hindu caste system. According to Hindu mores there should be no association between Brahmins and outcaste people. In fact, if the shadow of an outcaste should fall across a Brahmin, it would render him ceremonially unclean. But these two men were now close friends.

Mr. Paul, the Brahmin, had only recently become a Christian. It all began with a train ride. After boarding a train he found a copy of the Gospel of St. John lying on the seat that was assigned to him. He began to read. His interest ignited and he sought my missionary friend for instruction. As the instruction progressed his parents and other family relatives protested. And when Paul seemed to be moving toward accepting Christian baptism, relatives added threats of expulsion from the family; that would mean that he would be disinherited.

This created a radical soul struggle for Mr. Paul. Was family and property to be relinquished for the Christian faith? His decision to become a Christian prevailed. He announced it to the missionary with a joyous smile saying: "Now Christ means everything for me!"

I have inquired about Mr. Paul since I first met him. He entered the Lutheran Theological Seminary and was ordained a pastor. He chose to serve as a prison chaplain. Borrowing the book title of E. Stanley Jones, Mr. Paul sought to make "the Christ of the Indian Road" a Savior and Friend of those who were without friends.

My change in personal life-style was more than a change in mores. It extended also to the area of physical health.

Most young men just out of the seminary are eager to get at the parish work quickly and to try out some of the dreams and plans that were born when they were studying. I threw myself into the work from early morning until late in the evening. I developed a nervous stomach. After Sunday morning worship services, I would have to rest for an hour before eating—otherwise I could not retain my food; I was under a doctor's care, but nothing improved. I thought I might have to leave the ministry for a while and settle on a farm.

Then one day some new insights gripped my mind with impressive power. In prayer and reflection a sudden awareness dawned. I recognized that I dealt with my work as though it was primarily *my* work—as though the kingdom would arrive by the ideas and drive of Fred Schiotz. This awareness was followed by the recognition that the work belonged to the Lord long before it was mine. In that moment I could laugh at myself.

I let go of my possessive hold on the parish ministry. A holy leisure followed. Gradually new physical strength arrived. After some months God had made a new man of me. Since then, I have worked as hard as before but with less fatigue resulting. Fret and worry have not been allowed to add to the load that the body must carry. And I frequently savor the word of St. Paul to the Colossian Christians: "Let the peace of Christ rule in your hearts; to which indeed you were called in the one body. And be thankful!" (Col. 3:15).

3

THE PARISH YEARS

BEFORE ENTERING THE SEMINARY I taught high school for two years in my home town of Ladysmith. I knew I should like teaching; besides I had a small college indebtedness. Moreover, my younger brother was in high school, and I had promised my father to help him. These were rich years for me. Marshall Lewis, the superintendent, was most cooperative, and my friend, Mr. Dahlberg, was still on the faculty. I became the faculty advisor for the school's first annual, the *Flambeau Ripplings,* the sponsor for a newly organized Hi-Y group, and helped coach the debate team, in addition to my class load. As my second year came to a close, Mr. Lewis urged me to stay in teaching, but I reminded him of my commitment to the ministry. The senior class invited me to preach the baccalaureate sermon. My text was Jesus' words to his disciples, "Follow me" (Matt. 4:19).

My parish ministry was invested in three different congregations: Zion in Duluth, Minnesota, 1930-32; Trinity in Moorhead, Minnesota, 1932-38; Trinity in Brooklyn, New York, 1945-48.

A pastor is privileged to select his own text for the sermon he will preach at his installation service. In Duluth I selected the words of John the Baptist from the first chapter of the Gospel of John, verse 29b: "Behold, the Lamb of God, who takes away the sin of the world."

John was speaking to his disciples, directing attention away from himself with the focus on Jesus. To me, this epitomized the pastor's task. If he could get his parishioners to center attention on Jesus as the Sin Bearer and the Teacher, faith would become trust; insight into God's will would become action; and the preconditions for growth would be met. For me, this orientation of attitude was so compelling that I used the same text for the installation service at Moorhead and again in Brooklyn.

Zion had experienced some tension and bitterness and a split in the congregation had threatened. At the first congregational business meeting, I told the congregation that I had received a responsible briefing on what had happened. We would now make a new beginning and I would regard all people as members only—not as partisans of one side or the other. I asked as a matter of privilege that each member refrain from speaking to me about the controversy that had been. And if someone should forget my request and begin talking about the controversy that had been, I might embarrass them by walking away. No one forgot my request, and God blessed the congregation with a wholesome unity.

There was no one in the congregation who could assume responsibility for directing the choir. Since my wife had specialized in music at St. Olaf and had taken choral directing under Dr. Christiansen, she volunteered. This being our first parish, we agreed it should not become a habit. Where lay people in the congregation could do it or be trained for choir directing, the lay person should be given priority.

Since the senior choir was actually a youth choir, it became the core of our youth activity. The choir would often sing for shut-ins on a Sunday afternoon. Sometimes there would be a choral program for a neighboring congregation. Often such meetings would include picnics. While the meal was in preparation, the boys would play softball, the pastor participating. That became the nucleus of a parish softball team.

In devising a Sunday church school training program, it seemed desirable to invite other Lutheran congregations in the West End and West Duluth to cooperate. They said it had not been done before, but they were willing that it be tried. This work was supplemented by a congregational committee that worked to prepare a program of standards for teachers that was used in Zion. However, before it was put into effect, the teachers evaluated the program, criticized it and then approved it.

The cooperation in city church school teacher training led to selected joint festival worship services between Zion and two Augustana congregations, each no more than two blocks away.

It was suggested to the Arrowhead Circuit of the NLCA that a Circuit Luther League Bible Camp be organized for one week in the summer. Good facilities are important in such an effort. Camp Warren on the Range, a splendid Minneapolis YMCA Camp, was secured for a reasonable rental price. Circuit youth work received a lift through this effort.

Whenever standards are set for church school work, somewhere along the way, disciplinary problems may arise. One of the boys in my confirmation class, able but careless, repeatedly failed to hand in the written assignments. Finally, I had to announce that anyone who failed to get his work in would have to be bypassed and carried over into next year's class. Three weeks away from confirmation Sunday I had to advise the boy that he could not be confirmed that year.

As soon as the father got this word, he came to the parsonage in a belligerent and threatening mood. I showed him the boy's record. He recognized that it was very much deficient but insisted on confirmation that year. I told him that absence from class and lapses in the work are not a value subject to forgiveness. But if he, the father, would see to it that the son would meet me after school each day that remained before confirmation, I would tutor him. He agreed, the boy reported, and joined his class on confirmation Sunday. Thereafter, both father and son became warm friends of mine.

When illness or accident strike, the ministry takes a pastor to the very heart of his calling. During such times he is always a learner as well as a ministrant. A few occasions may illustrate.

The first fall I was called to the hospital to minister to a man who was in a coma. Is there a point in trying to communicate to someone who for all purposes seems to have lost consciousness—except to ease the burden on relatives? I decided to pray as though the man would understand. But in doing so I held his hand. As I prayed there was an unmistakable response. His fingers pressed my hand, ever so slightly, but it could not be misunderstood. It was repeated several times. I have never since hesitated to pray in the presence of a person reputed to be in a coma.

One Sunday morning the same fall, news came in that a teenager had been killed instantly in an automobile crash. Busy with a number of appointments, I sent word that I would call on the parents in the afternoon. How does one serve in such a moment? A beloved son, on the threshhold of life, is suddenly taken from you. This was a family whose acquaintance I had not yet made.

When I entered the home, I expressed my sympathy to the parents in the tragic loss they had sustained. After that there did not seem to be anything more to say—unless the parents opened the door for conversation. But they sat in mute stillness—as though in a stupor. I sat and in silence prayed for them. As late afternoon gave way to darkness, since I had another appointment to keep, I asked whether I should conduct devotions before leaving. Their answer welcomed it, and suddenly they became aware that we were sitting in darkness. A table lamp was turned on. A short Scripture and prayer followed in the Norwegian language. I bade good night and promised to call again. It seemed to me that I had failed them in their hour of need.

After the funeral this couple began to attend church regularly whereas before it had been on occasional special Sundays. By the grapevine I heard that they had told friends how much my Sunday afternoon call had meant to them. Then I learned that we were not alone in our ministry. The Paraclete is at our side and he also uses silence for communication. Too much chatter can block transmission of meaning.

During the week between Christmas and New Year, I was called to a home where the grandfather was sick with a terminal illness. After some conversation and prayer, I asked whether he would like a home communion service. He indicated he would like it, but did not dare ask for it—for "I am not worthy." I had come to recognize that many people of Norwegian or Danish extraction who had received their catechetical instruction through the use of the Danish Bishop Pontoppidan's Explanation of Luther's Catechism thought this way. It was a good book, but Pontoppidan placed a disproportionate emphasis on St. Paul's warning to Corinthian Christians (1 Cor. 11:17-22, 27-29). Paul found a situation where the love feasts were characterized by segregation of the rich from the poor, and some drank sacramental wine to the point of intoxication. It was then that the apostle warned that they would be eating and drinking *judgment* on themselves. If this context is not remembered, St. Paul's words may drive people away from the communion table.

I turned to my parishioner and inquired whether he had given any Christmas gifts to his grandchildren. He replied in the affirmative. "Suppose," I said, "you should find that your grandchildren had not even opened your gift packages."

"I would not like that. Likely, I would not want to give them a gift again," he answered.

He had opened the door for a direct word from me. And So I asked, "Why do you insist on keeping the gift Christ gave us in holy communion wrapped up in a package lying on the shelf unused?" He saw the point at once, smiled, and asked me to arrange so that he could be communed.

Long before I came to Duluth, a member of the congregation was suspended because of his alcoholism. It angered the man, and he responded in kind by resigning from membership in the congregation. Thereafter he had no use for the church. While we were in Duluth, he suffered a massive stroke, lost his speech, and became a bed patient in the home of his daughter. She paid me a visit, explained the background, and concluded by asking if I would call on him. However, she warned that I might get an unhappy reception.

When I called I found him propped up in bed, half reclining. The only way in which I could converse was by asking simple questions which could be answered by a nod of the head or the incoherent mumbling of a short phrase. I asked if he would like me to conduct devotions for him. There was no answer. I therefore proceeded. Slowly he raised himself up on one elbow; with the other arm he made a crude effort to knock the New Testament out of my hand. I stopped at once. I then announced that I would have to go, but told him that I would call again the next day.

The second visit was a repetition of the first. I left wondering how this wounded spirit could be reached. As I walked and thought about it, an inner certainty developed that if I could carry him back to his early years of life, the barrier he had erected might be pierced.

When I returned home I proposed to my wife that she accompany me the next day. I would introduce her to him and thereafter she could step back and stand at the foot of the bed. If he should again become aggressively hostile, I would look at her. Without further ado she should begin to sing a Norwegian hymn that we knew he would have heard frequently in childhood.

With a prayer in our hearts, we were back the next day. He reacted as he had done before. My wife began to sing. Suddenly he stopped the effort to reach my New Testament. His eyes became transfixed on my wife as though he were hearing a voice from another world. As he listened I noted some tear drops gathering in his eyes. Suddenly he fell back on his pillows and began to sob like a child. Prayer followed. I asked if he would like me to arrange a communion service for him. His mumbling reply could not be mistaken as anything other than yes.

I came back the next afternoon. Once again my wife accompanied me and sang a few liturgical responses. He was a happy participant in that service. Never again was there objection to hearing God's Word. A couple of months later he died trusting in the Lord who had adopted him in Holy Baptism.

One of the senior citizens who always attended a Norwegian service was a very thoughtful bachelor. He listened with an intentness so that you could almost hear the cerebral wheels turning. He was widely read. If he had had the formal education, he might well have been a theological professor. I learned much in my conversations with him. One day his landlady sent word that he was ill and wanted to see me. He had been stricken with pneumonia. After some conversation and prayer, he gave me a sealed envelope, asking that it be opened when I got the news of his death.

In that envelope he requested me to use the text he had chosen for his funeral service. And this was it: "The saying is sure and worthy of full acceptance, that Christ Jesus came into the world to save sinners. And I am the foremost of sinners" (1 Tim. 1:15). It was sheer joy to preach that funeral sermon.

In 1932 Moorhead was a city of about 8000 people. Fargo, a much larger city and the ranking metropolis of North Dakota, was contiguous, except for the Red River that flowed between them.

Moorhead was a community of two colleges: Concordia College, a school of the Evangelical Lutheran Church (ELC), formerly called the Norwegian Lutheran Church; the second was a state institution, then known as the Moorhead State Teachers College.

Concordia had about 500 students at that time. Not long after my arrival I was elected a member of the board of directors. Dr. J. N. Brown, president of the college, invited me to speak at chapel several times and then suggested that I should make it a weekly visit to the campus. In accepting I announced that we would make weekly observation walks in the Book of Job.

Student attendance at Sunday church services was excellent. Trinity Church could comfortably accommodate 750 people; if crowded, approximately 900 people. Two English services were held each Sunday morning. About half of those who attended were students, most of them from Concordia but a number also from MSTC. It was almost like facing a youth convention each Sunday that I entered the pulpit.

Three pastors who had been friends of mine since college days joined with me as a team to assist some of our church colleges in an annual "Christian emphasis week." I inquired of Dr. Brown if he would like the team to visit the Concordia campus. Since I was on the local scene, I would serve as liaison but would not do any of the speaking during the week. I told him that the three visiting speakers would be Dr. B. M. Christensen of Augsburg College, Dr. L. M. Stavig, pastor of St. John's in Northfield, and the Rev. Arthur Johnson, pastor of Ezekiel Lutheran Church in River Falls, Wisconsin, and chaplain to Lutheran students at River Falls Teachers College. Dr. Brown welcomed the suggestion.

When the week was over, one of the senior girls asked for a conference. In our conversation I discovered that she was from Pennsylvania and had never been baptized. She announced that she wanted to become a Christian and wished to prepare for baptism. I wondered whether this girl would accept public baptism. When the time came for this decision, without any hesitance, she chose to be baptized in the presence of her whole class on baccalaureate Sunday.

The enrollment of students at Moorhead State Teachers College was about the same as at Concordia. And about half of these students were Lutheran. I told the Board of Deacons at Trinity that I thought we had a responsibility for these students. If the board approved, I would, with assistance of some MSTC faculty who also were members of Trinity, organize a Lutheran Student Association group. The board approved of this extension of ministry.

One day a nurse inquired of my wife whether there was any Lutheran service on a Sunday evening in Moorhead. She explained that her work hours prevented her from getting to any Sunday morning worship. My wife answered that as far as she knew, there was no Sunday evening Protestant services; but she would report the nurse's concern to me. I reported this inquiry to the board of deacons. I volunteered to assume responsibility for an evening schedule. The board approved but warned that the work load might be too heavy. And so, Sunday evening services were begun.

The economic effects of the depression, increased by the general drought in the Great Plains area, caused great concern for church officials and pastors of congregations. In the winter months of 1934 I wondered whether Trinity would be able to meet its full mission quota to the synod. Several of our trustees were critical of our high allocation.

I had to grant that the trustees had a valid point. There should be a reexamination of the allocation process through the proper channels, but not by rebellion. I had been considering a proposal of directing the congregation's attention to bring in a victory offering for mission on Easter Sunday. I submitted the plan to the trustees and concluded by asking if it would not be better to lead than to further emphasize the gloom of that day. They examined the plan and after considerable discussion authorized it to be carried out. Some may have voted "with tongue in cheek."

Lent was begun by announcing that we were going to focus on an Easter Victory offering for missions. We dispensed with collections at the midweek Lenten services. Instead, at each Lenten service people were encouraged to pray for a willing and glad response of our people on Easter. Anticipation began to build up. A letter went out to all members at the beginning of Holy Week. Suggested specifics were a part of that letter. For many without work there was encouragement not to be ashamed of a small gift—or even no gift—everything was to be done with prayer and gladness of heart.

The financial secretary and his enlarged staff of helpers were busy opening envelopes and counting all Easter Sunday afternoon. The telephone at the parsonage rang frequently that afternoon. And each one who called inquired, "How did the Easter offering go?" When the afternoon was over, it was possible to say that God had moved our people to place on the altar the largest offering in the congregation's history. Then were the people of Trinity glad (John 20:20b).

During the spring of my first year, it seemed desirable to organize a week of Bible camp for our own youth. For this purpose we rented a property on Lake Tulaby near Mahnomen, Minnesota. The charge for each youth was $3 for the week, $1 for rent of the camp and $2 for food. This was supplemented a little by gifts in kind. At the close of the week so many good reports reached parents from their own children that requests came in asking that such a week be a part of each summer.

Plans were then projected for the next summer. It became clear that the owner of the property at Lake Tulaby regarded satisfied customers as people who would willingly pay an increase in rental charges. We felt that we had to hold the costs at $3 per person per week because of the times. We began looking for property where we would be our own landlord.

One day Mr. S. G. Reinertson, superintendent of schools, told me that a book salesman had spoken to him about a property that was available at Menahga, Minnesota, 90 miles from Moorhead. It was an 80-acre tract of land and water, 30 acres of water were enclosed by 50 acres of forest. I answered Mr. Reinertson, "That sounds like a glorified frog pond."

I invested two weeks of my vacation camping on the property. I wrote letters to all ELC pastors in the Northern Minnesota District who had shown interest in Bible camp work for their youth. I announced the option to buy for $1600. I suggested that they join Pastor Agnar Tanner of Ulen, Minnesota (who had already declared in favor of acquiring the property for camp work), and me at Menahga on Labor Day, the first week in September. It is my recollection that about 12 men showed up. All were enthusiastic about the possibilities of the property. But one after another said this was no time to consider building. After the meeting only Tanner and I were left—unwilling to give up.

As we prayed and thought about the project, an inner certainty gripped us that there would be a way out. We knew we could not place the matter before our congregations; the economic depression would not permit it. Finally, we found a way out by organizing an independent self-perpetuating corporation whose trustees had to be members of Trinity Lutheran Church and the Ulen parish. Thus, the congregations were not obligated, but the values of the camp accrued for their work.

It was remarkable how the Lord opened up doors to people who were willing to lend money, some of it without interest obligations. Mr. Miller, businessmen in Menahga, and a lady who held a mortgage on the property donated $235—thus making the net purchasing price for the land $1365.

There were many corners turned while Camp Emmaus was being erected. When we thought there would be a problem after the next turn in the road, God was always ahead of us to meet our need. On dedication day after four weeks of use that summer, I said to a few who remained after the service, "To me this was hallowed ground even before our dedication today. In so many ways God has shown us that he willed this facility for a ministry to youth. We stand on holy ground!"

From time to time I had heard people complain that pastors are so busy that it is almost impossible to get to see them. That pastors in large congregations are busy is true enough. But a way must be found whereby people can reach them for such pastoral counsel as people may wish. To help make this possible, I announced to Trinity that every Thursday evening from 7:00 o'clock on I would be in my study available to anyone who would come or ask. I allowed nothing to interfere with this schedule (unless I had to be out of the city), and I have never regretted that I committed myself to this program.

When we first arrived in Moorhead, a mother in the congregation called to tell me that she had a married daughter who had demitted the church to join the Christian Scientists. At one time she had been very active in Trinity, and therefore the daughter's leaving troubled her mother that much more. She asked me to keep her daughter in mind. I promised that I would do so but reminded the mother that this was a situation where we would have to wait for the Holy Spirit to prepare the way.

Two years later the mother became seriously ill. I called at the daughter's home where the mother then lived. After I had visited with the mother and conducted devotions, the daughter followed me out on the veranda. There she began timidly, "I suppose you know that I am a Christian Scientist?"

I answered, "Yes."

Then she added, a trifle defiantly, "I was healed from a serious illness!"

"Yes, I believe you," I replied. "What's more, I believe God healed you." This apparent approval piqued her curiosity, but nothing more was said that day.

Short visits with the daughter took place each time I called on the mother. One day I took time to elaborate a little on what I had been saying in bits and pieces. I called her attention to the way in which much illness is brought on by the multiplied forms in which emotional disturbance afflicts us. Illness thus induced responds to Christian Science treatment. When this happens it is because the patient has relaxed to the degree that the strong recuperative powers God has placed in the body are allowed to work. It is as though the brakes that are put on the body by worry, hatred, resentments, etc., are released. This happens also for Christians, who daily—or from hour to hour—allow the peace of Christ to rule in their heart (Col. 3:15).

But there is a chasm of separation between Christian Science and Christian faith. Christian Science says that illness is not real; it is imagined. Christian faith looks at the ugliest things in life and identifies them: illness is real; sin is real. But God's forgiveness in Christ is greater than the sin that readily besets us. And if we allow the peace of Christ to rule in our hearts, it induces therapy.

The day of the mother's funeral, I rode back from the cemetery with the funeral director. He was both a neighbor, friend, and a member of Trinity. He turned to me and said, "Pastor, if you would now invite the daughter to return to Trinity, I think she is ready to come."

"I would gladly do so," I answered. "But she walked out of the church on her own decision. She must return in the same way. In other words, her choice must be made in freedom with no taint of coercion."

When I left Trinity, I briefed my successor on what had transpired in this lady's life. I wanted him to be prepared to minister to her when the time would come.

A year after I had left Moorhead, I was back on a special mission. While walking toward the church, whom should I see coming toward me but the former Christian Scientist. When she saw me her face broke out in a big smile. And she joyfully announced, "I am back in Trinity." A storm-tossed craft had reached the harbor in safety.

Trinity Lutheran Church at Fourth Avenue and Forty-sixth Street in Brooklyn was organized in 1890. Thus it was younger than most congregations in the Midwest. The immigrants from Norway during the latter part of the 19th century and the early part of the 20th gravitated to the large cities. A considerable colony of Norwegians settled in Brooklyn.

These people were largely from the southwestern part of Norway. This is the part of Norway that provides heavy support for world missions and for much inter-mission activity. The Christian life is characterized by warmth, fervor, and prayer.

Trinity was a large congregation, very low church in its worship style. In 1945 there was still a strong demand for Norwegian in worship services. In fact, there were practically two congregations in one, with one board of trustees and two boards of deacons. At this time the Norwegian division always met in the sanctuary on Sunday morning. The American division met in the chapel (church basement).

I found a great reservoir of active Christian lay people in Trinity. The Sunday school teaching staff had actually realized a goal I held before the congregations in Duluth and Moorhead: 50% of the teachers were men. Harold Midtbo, the Sunday school superintendent, had done graduate work in education that he might be a better educator in the church school.

The congregation's membership roll was not as large as I had surmised, probably between 700 and 800. But there were a number who participated in one or another phase of Trinity's life whose names were not on the church roll. The giving was very good. The congregation provided a staff of one pastor to assist in the Norwegian division, one to assist in the American division, two office secretaries, and a part-time deaconess.

I had had occasion to observe that a multiple staff may contribute to unnecessary tension in a congregation. I vowed that this must not happen in Trinity. But the determination was not enough. There would also have to be the right kind of staff structure. All staff members were assigned specific areas of responsibility. Aside from major policy questions, staff members were free to plan and to do what they thought best in carrying out their assignments of responsibility. Perquisites for pastoral acts were pooled. At the end of the month they were divided equally.

Once every week we held a staff meeting. The custodian was also invited, but his European background made him embarrassed about joining us. Information that should be known by each staff member was shared. Criticisms and suggestions for the work were placed before the group. We concluded with free prayer in which each participated; often it would center in intercession for the work of the congregation, particularly the sick.

The congregations' low church liturgical practices did not allow for the use of vestments. I found a bylaw to the constitution which specified: *Presten skal ikke ha Klaer* (the constitution had not yet been translated into English). Literally interpreted, this phrase meant, "The pastor shall not have clothes"; but its idiomatic meaning was simply, "The pastor shall not use vestments."

I prefer to use liturgical vestments, and I told the congregation that this was my preference. However, the bylaw specification did not bother me to the degree that I was uncomfortable functioning in a street suit. Paul's reasoning in Romans 14 is applicable also in a matter of this kind.

Sister Ingeborg had served Trinity most of her life as a deaconess. She was now slipping in her physical strength. She did some calling and she was the guardian of the congregation's membership roll. This was an assignment that Dr. S. O. Sigmond, who served the congregation for more than 25 years, had given her. As strength began to fail, she was doubly jealous of her assignment, probably because she knew it was not complete and hoped to bring it up to date.

In discussing this matter with the deacons, it was agreed that we had to ease this out of her care, and make the membership roll a matter of public record. I suggested to Sister Ingeborg that she prepare the roster of members as she believed it to be. This we circulated in the congregation and asked those whose names did not appear but believed themselves to be members to declare their evidence. There were rectifications to be made but people were patient; there was great appreciation for the many-sided rich ministry Sister Ingeborg had carried out over the years.

Some humorous situations arose. For those who believed themselves to be members but for whom there was no record, we held a Sunday evening membership reception service. Just before this service began, Sister Ingeborg brought information to me that showed one member who was to be received that evening had actually been a member for many years. One of the ushers asked the man to step into the sacristy. I told him about the new record found by Sister Ingeborg and that it would not therefore be necessary for him to be received anew. He refused to step aside. He wanted to go through with the reception service that it might be publicly witnessed that he had been received into the fellowship of the congregation. "I don't want that there should be any mistake about it this time," he said. I marveled at his refusal to be insulted by the error that had been made and his perseverance in making sure that no new mistake should be made. After this service a public record of the membership roll was reported and thereafter the records were kept by the secretaries in the office.

Along with this reform in the record keeping, the constitution was translated from Norwegian to English.

Trinity had a multiplicity of meetings, from scout groups and choirs to mission groups, prayer meetings and study and discussion groups. It is the only congregation that I have found where there was a tradition of Bible and topical study discussion groups on Saturday evenings. And it never seemed to interfere with church attendance on Sunday mornings. To keep the many meetings each week off a collision course in the use of church facilities, it seemed well to initiate a late spring planning conference. This brought together the leaders of all groups for a weekend retreat. Plans for the ensuing year were made. Conflicts were reconciled and a master plan was recorded. This was transposed to a church calendar beginning with September and concluding the following August. This calendar was sent to each member of the congregation. It became a very valuable tool.

While I was serving the American Lutheran Conference in student work, I was frequently disturbed to see how little Lutherans knew about the Augsburg Confession. Since this is the basic theological document of the Lutheran church, it seemed to me that it ought to be better known and understood by our people. I promised myself that if I ever went back to serve in a parish, I would look for an opportunity to bring it to the attention of the people.

After I had been in Trinity for a while, the resolve I had made came to mind. The Sunday evening services were song services with topical material for the sermons. It seemed to me that this would be an appropriate time for a discussion of the Augsburg Confession. I decided to deal with one article each evening, giving each article a topical focus. Because many people have an a priori attitude that doctrine is dry, uninteresting material, I made special effort to place window illustrations in my sermons.

The first Sunday evening I seemed to have an interested, responsive congregation. But then during the week the grapevine brought news of many objections to so much attention being devoted to doctrinal discussions. These reports led me to say the second Sunday evening that I had heard there were many objections to my centering the Sunday evening sermons in the Augsburg Confession. I then said, "Why don't we talk it over?" And I announced the midweek meeting would be devoted to a hearing on the issue.

When the midweek meeting came, the turnout was better than at any other such meeting while I was in Brooklyn. I explained to the group the background for my decision to preach on our great Reformation "Magna Charta." When this had been done, the floor was thrown open for questions and discussion. What was said was pretty well summarized in the statement of a young man that could be paraphrased as follows: "You see, Pastor, we are not saying that you have not preached the Word of God. But we have a tradition in Trinity that our emphasis should be on life rather than doctrine. And we do not want to lose this tradition."

I suggested that it might be helpful to conduct a straw advisory vote. *Yes* would mean that I should continue what I had started. *No* would be their suggestion that I should drop the Augsburg Confession lectures. The vote was by ballot.

When the ballots had been counted, they were overwhelmingly negative. I then said to the group, "In a sense, no pastor should allow the congregation to dictate what to preach as long as he is faithful to the Word of God. But there is no purpose in preaching if people sit with their ears closed. I am therefore going to honor your advisory vote. But I hope that a day may come when you will of your own accord ask me to return to a discussion of the Augsburg Confession."

After the meeting one man lingered. He was from the Norwegian Division; but because his wife was in the American Division, he often came to American Division meetings. With a sorrowful voice, he expressed regret at the outcome of the vote. Then he observed: "If you had never said anything about the Augsburg Confession, but had merely announced a series of topics, each dealing with an article of the confession, there would have been no criticism. In fact, I think they would have been pleased with the sermon series."

When I returned home from that meeting, I told my wife what had transpired. Her reaction was given in a question: "Do you think you had a right to let them vote, even though you called it an advisory vote, on what you are to preach?"

I replied, "I let go to get a better hold."

The Sunday school had for many years been pushing the walls out at Trinity. Dr. Sigmond placed his heavy emphasis on having an adequate corps of pastors and other workers. Buildings were always a lesser concern for him. And one must admit that his emphasis had produced remarkable results. The people came in large numbers and many were brought into a lively awareness of discipleship. When the call committee visited with me, they made it clear that I would be expected to lead the congregation into an awareness that they must "rise up and build" (Neh. 2:18b) a very much needed educational building.

We began with the organization of a building committee with the necessary assisting committees. We knew that a massive education campaign would be required. And this had to be done in such a way that no one would be fearful about asking questions. This resulted in a decision to have a series of cottage meetings, two each evening for a period of one month, Sundays alone excepted. I committed myself to attend each cottage meeting.

In one of the meetings an engineer in one of the coastal boats announced that he did not believe in pledging. "How do I know that I will be living at the end of the three years for which the pledge is to be made?" I replied that all of life is based on promises and commitments. "How does your shipping firm know that it will still be in business at the end of the month to pay the salary it has pledged you?" He saw that he himself was the recipient of many commitments that various commercial firms had made to him.

The Easter Sunday offering brought an answer to the prayers of many and a satisfying reward to the building committee and all its workers. Months afterward, the engineer who said that he did not believe in pledging sought me out and confessed that the whole effort had been for him a stirring spiritual experience in which he had been richly blessed.

When the men and women came back from the war, church attendance grew rapidly in the American Division. The chapel (basement) became crowded. Chairs placed in the aisles bordered on violation of the fire department's regulations. It was clear that something had to be done.

In a discussion in the American Board of Deacons, they concluded the only solution was to move the American service into the sanctuary, and the Norwegian service downstairs in the chapel. It was proposed that it be recommended to the annual meeting. It was assured of passing because the American section would have more votes in the annual meeting. Someone then made the wise observation that even though the American section would win in the voting, we might actually lose in the amount of ill will that would follow. The Norse section would consider it ruthless preemption.

I suggested that we bring the situation to the attention of the annual meeting with a recommendation that we refer it to the Norwegian Division for their decision. One deacon replied, "Pastor, you don't know how set some of those people are."

I replied, "Let them have the joy of volunteering."

The following Sunday, I had the sermon in the Norwegian Division. I made it short, and then resolved the service into a business meeting. I explained how young people, and particularly those returning from military service, were crowding the chapel for the American service. We needed more room badly. The Norwegian Division did not fill the sanctuary and could be accommodated in the chapel with some room to spare.

I went on to say that no decision should be made that day. It would be too easy to say that "Pastor Schiotz decided it for us." I urged them to go home and from time to time during the week to pray about it. I advised them not to talk with neighbors about it, only to God. Then to come the next Sunday prepared to vote.

When a business meeting of the Norwegian Division was convened after the next Sunday's service, opportunity was provided for questions. Thereafter the people voted by ballot. When the votes had been counted, it was overwhelmingly in favor of moving down into the chapel. An usher told me about one of the older ladies in the congregation who had to leave immediately after the balloting. When she passed him, tears were streaming down her face and she said, "I didn't want to, I didn't want to; but I had to, I had to." I am sure she voiced the struggle that many had fought.

The American Division was astounded at the result, and the Norwegian Division was blessed in the conviction that they had laid a precious value on the altar for the kingdom's sake. The entire congregation continued throughout the year to be blessed with a special quality of unity.

When I got home after the service I said to my wife, "Today I collected a dividend on my willingness to accept defeat on the Augsburg Confession issue." The pastor who will accept defeat graciously, may find that it paves the road on which he can move forward to other kingdom victories.

I had been at Trinity three years when the officers of the ELC and the chairman of the Board of World Missions prevailed on me to accept a call as the executive secretary of the Commission on Younger Churches and Orphaned Missions of the U.S. Committee of the Lutheran World Federation. The three years in Brooklyn were a different type of experience than the service in Duluth and Moorhead. The people of Trinity had strong convictions about their Christian faith. But sometimes these convictions were overlayed with fears of ecclesiastical formalism to a degree that almost became an addiction. I once told them in a congregational meeting, "Your concern for low churchly practices has become a new type of formalism for you." They smiled in recognition that this could easily come to be.

My continuing image of Trinity is that of many stalwart men and women of faith. I could always be sure that they were upholding me with their intercession and good will.

4

IN THE WAKE OF WORLD WAR II

WHEN WORLD WAR II BROKE OUT, Lutherans in the Scandinavian countries and in North America were mobilized for action. In 1941 the National Lutheran Council churches raised $500,000, one-half to support the Service Commission (a ministry to Lutherans in the armed forces), and the balance for orphaned missions and war refugees. It was clear that much more money would be required. Under the name *Lutheran World Action* almost $80,000,000 was raised in the next 14 years.

This money was invested to aid many thousands of people in 75 countries around the world. A National Lutheran Council sponsored sister organization called Lutheran World Relief served both the NLC churches and the Lutheran Church—Missouri Synod in providing material relief. LWR literally fed and clothed thousands of hungry and naked people who had been dispossessed by war and its attendant evils.

Orphaned Missions

In the Scandinavian countries and in Germany world missionary outreach was done almost entirely by independent missionary societies. Few people, unacquainted with Germany, would believe that there could be as many missionary societies as the German Christians supported. World War II cut the mission societies of Denmark, Norway, and Germany off from the areas in the world where they had been at work. Thus the term "orphaned missions" came into use.

In this situation the International Missionary Council, with offices in London and New York, proceeded to organize Protestant churches for action. While the war was on, the IMC looked to the Lutheran World Convention to initiate support for the Lutheran orphaned missions. This was carried out through the Church of Sweden in cooperation with the National Lutheran Council.

After the war something more than emergency help had to be provided for the orphaned missions. In 1947 the constituting convention of the Lutheran World Federation met in Lund, Sweden. This was the first international church consultation after the war years. It called on Lutheran churches to launch a ministry of rehabilitation and healing for the homeless brethren of Europe and help for her war-battered churches. Alongside of this call was a stirring summons to assist the foreign mission societies and their emerging churches.

This call led the United States Committee of the LWF (the same personnel that constituted the Executive Committee of the NLC) to organize a Commission on Younger Churches and Orphaned Missions; usually referred to as CYCOM. The inclusion of the words Younger Churches in the name of the commission was a signal to the churches in mission areas that they were to be consulted in all policy actions.

CYCOM elected me its executive secretary. When this news

reached me I sought a conference with Dr. Fry, chairman of the commission. I told him that in my judgment the commission should have elected someone who was at home in the German language. I got a typical Fry response: "It is time the Germans learn English." And so, I took office August 1, 1948. Never did the German mission directors make me feel uncomfortable because of my inability to speak German.

Later in 1948 the LWF authorized the organization of a Federation Commission on World Mission (CWM, pronounced koom). I was appointed chairman of the commission. Its formal organization meeting was held at Oxford, England, in the summer of 1949.

During the six years of my serving CYCOM I never waved the American flag. Always I spoke of the work as something being done by the entire Lutheran family under the auspices of the Lutheran World Federation—even though most of the supporting funds were given by the NLC churches.

The fascinating story of CYCOM's work during the years 1948-54 was too many-sided to make these pages a proper historical record. This may be found in the scores of agendas, minutes, and the reams of correspondence. But there were experiences of God's providence that stirred the blood, and other experiences that revealed some heroic German mission leaders, and some stalwart indigenous leaders in the third world churches. Some of these action events and vignettes must be shared with the people of the church.

I start with Africa.

The IMC London Consultation

In June 1948 (actually two months before I fully assumed my CYCOM responsibilities), the IMC sponsored a consultation of Protestant mission directors whose boards carried on work in Africa. German mission directors with similar responsibilities were included. The purpose was to consult with one another and to meet British secretaries from the Africa section in the Colonial office. At that time Sir Andrew Cohen was in charge of the Africa section.

Three impressions remain from that consultation:

1) The apparent timidity of the German representatives as though they wondered whether the hospitality of the IMC and the friendliness of the other mission directors could be accepted at face value.

2) The readiness of the Colonial Office to share information and to answer questions. The exchange of information was largely related to Colonial Office policies in the several areas of Africa for which they carried responsibility.

3) The great fund of information that the mission directors had regarding the areas wherein their boards were at work. They seemed at times to be better informed than the government men. Dr. Emory Ross, the executive secretary for the Africa Committee of the National Council of Churches in the USA, was a known expert on Africa. By the questions he asked and his input in the discussions, it became obvious to Sir Andrew Cohen that here was a man with encyclopedic knowledge about all of Africa. He invited Dr. Ross to be his guest over the weekend. When Dr. Ross returned to the conference on Monday morning he told of having been hosted at Mr. Cohen's summer home. In the visiting much of the time had been spent in answering the probing questions of his host.

Since that London consultation there have been many other opportunities to observe that it is not unusual that servants of the church may be better informed about overseas human relations problems than servants of the state.

The German Evangelical Missionary Council

In September 1948 I had my first opportunity to become better acquainted with the German mission directors. I had the privilege of being a guest at the annual meeting of the German Evangelical Missionary Council. Eight major foreign mission organizations plus a grouping of small specialty societies, were represented by their respective staffs. Some professors of mission were also present. A few of the delegates were from the DDR (East Germany). We met at a Reformed Theological Seminary in Herborn in the Rhineland.

Some insights gained at the Herborn meeting have never been forgotten:

1) I got a new impression of Luther. In the room that served as dining room and meeting hall, there was a picture of a Reformation leader on each of the four walls. On one was a small picture of John Calvin. On each of the other walls the pictures were larger and they were all of Luther. And this was a Reformed Seminary! It was then that I discovered that Luther is not only a great leader in the church, but he is also a national hero in Germany—not unlike a George Washington for us.

2) Although it was three years since World War II fighting had stopped, there was plenty of evidence that the hardships imposed by the war still lingered. The staple for each meal seemed to be some form of potato. Even the "coffee" breaks might provide potato soup.

The pipe smoking that went on after a meal and during the conference sessions was difficult to accept. There was none of the pleasant aroma provided by choice tobacco blends. Alas, there were no tobaccos to be blended. The only tobacco to be had was what each smoker had raised in the family vegetable garden.

3) Professor Walter Freytag of the University of Hamburg was the chairman of the Missionary Council. Few men in the 20th century could match Professor Freytag in his knowledge of world missionary activity and his understanding of the problems that had to be faced. It was clear that he was the confidant of the mission directors.

4) In Professor Freytag's chairmanship, I saw parliamentary

procedure, European style, in action. He announced the agenda item to be discussed, allowed discussion to continue until consensus seemed to be emerging. He would often hasten the process by well-directed questions. Instead of calling for a formal vote, he announced the outcome of debate. He could be challenged, but it rarely happened; happy acceptance of his decisions was the rule. There is something to be said for this informal procedure as over against our regularized use of motions, made and seconded, and then voted.

5) One of the important reasons for my presence at Herborn was to provide information to the German mission directors on how CYCOM's help would be administered. I emphasized that we would need a lot of factual information about each society's work and their own evaluation of priorities. Only then could CYCOM make decisions that would be reasonably fair to the work of each society. After I had spoken and had answered questions, Director August Elfers of the Hermannsburg Mission Society rose to make a Hermannsburg policy statement which I paraphrase as follows: "Hermannsburg has never made known its needs to anyone. It is our policy to tell God about our needs, and he provides. For this reason we cannot give you the information you have requested."

This trusting child-like faith might seem naive; but there was no pious exhibitionism intended. The Hermannsburg constituency was nurtured in its Christian commitments through the Bible study-mission movement of its founder, the beloved Pastor Ludwig Harms. If you were to visit Hermannsburg in northern Germany today, you would find Bible passages painted on the exterior walls of many of the homes.

How was I to respond to Director Elfers' policy statement without surrendering my responsibilities to CYCOM and the donors of Lutheran World Action funds? Care had to be taken not to bruise the trusting faith out of which Director Elfers spoke.

I began my reply by addressing him as "Brother Elfers." Then I proceeded to speak soberly and deliberately: "The money over which CYCOM has custody is not our money, nor is it any longer the money of the donors. It is God's money. CYCOM is God's steward, appointed to use the money wisely and well—so that we may give a good account of our stewardship. Brother Elfers, place yourself in CYCOM's position. How could you possibly distribute these gift funds without a maximum amount of information. Certainly, we are praying about it. In fact, my being here is a part of God's answer to your prayers. He has led us to seek facts about the need from you and from your fellow mission directors. Surely, you will not deny us the facts we need to do a responsible work with God's money."

With a smile Director Elfers replied, "We will cooperate."

6) Some of the directors represented mission societies that had their headquarters offices in the DDR. They laid before their fellow directors their great difficulty in sending any money at all out of their country. Government restrictions did not permit it. The Leipzig Mission Society asked: "What can be done?"

Whenever there are complicated issues to be faced, someone is usually ready to present a simple solution which often solves nothing. And so it was during this discussion. A West German delegate proposed that Leipzig move its headquarters office to West Germany; there would then be no restrictions in sending money out of the country.

The speaker had no more than finished his statement, when Director Carl Ihmels of the Leipzig Mission Society jumped out of his chair as though he might have been jabbed by a needle. He literally shouted: "No! God has placed me in Leipzig to be his light there!"

This moving declaration took on added eloquence and theological insight when I learned what had happened in the Ihmels' home. They had a son who had been an active Christian youth worker. He was loved by the young people. Authoritarian governments are always afraid of those who have acceptance among the youth. Late one night the secret police knocked on the door of the Ihmels' home. They placed the son under arrest and took him away. The parents could get no information about what had been done with their son. And they did not see him again until he was returned home in a coffin. It was the father in this home who said, "God has placed me in Leipzig to be his light there!"

Tanganyika

The primary Africa area for CYCOM's attention was Tanganyika. Once it had been German East Africa. After World War I East Africa was placed under the supervision of the League of Nations. The League made it a mandated territory to be administered by Great Britain. After World War II the mandate was renewed, and Great Britain was made responsible to the United Nations.

Three German mission societies had initiated work in Tanganyika, receiving large grants of land from the German government for schools, churches, and other purposes related to ministering to the people. These societies were Berlin, Bethel, and Leipzig. Each one had been assigned responsibilities for working in two areas of the country. Berlin was given responsibility for the Dar-es-Salaam and Southern Highlands regions. Bethel was assigned the Tanga area with the contiguous Usambara Mountain region, and the province of Bukoba on the western shore of Lake Victoria. Leipzig worked in Central Tanganyika and in the northern part in the Kilimanjaro and Pare Mountain districts.

After World War I Leipzig relinquished its responsibilities in Central Tanganyika to the Augustana Evangelical Lutheran Church of the USA. However, it continued its work in northern Tanganyika. Berlin and Bethel returned to administer work on their two respective fields. The three societies carried on their work with diligence until World War II broke out.

The Lutheran World Convention, in consultation with the National Lutheran Council, arranged to have the Board of World Mission of Augustana assume supervision of the five orphaned fields during World War II. Augustana was assisted by the Church of Sweden Mission in Bukoba and the Swedish Evangelical Society in the Southern Highlands. A field Administrative Committee for the orphaned missions work was organized with Dr. George N. Anderson of Augustana as the administrative director.

When CYCOM was organized the Augustana Board made it known that it would expect to be relieved of administrative supervision for the orphaned areas. CYCOM accepted the transfer, acknowledging that its assigned responsibilities covered such action.

At the outset of World War II, the British Custodian of Enemy Properties had seized all properties belonging to the three German societies. Permits for the use of the church and school buildings had to be sought by Augustana and renewed from year to year. Dr. Hjalmar Swanson, the executive director of the Augustana Board, advised CYCOM that an early effort should be made to secure a release of the German mission society properties and permission for German missionaries to return to Tanganyika. This therefore became a task of prior importance on my first visit to Tanganyika.

On my way to Tanganyika I stopped off in London to call on Sir Andrew Cohen. I thought a word from him might be useful in talking with the Tanganyika officials. But Mr. Cohen was coy about giving any advice. He said that all authority for action with regard to enemy properties was in the hands of the Tanganyika government.

Dr. George Anderson had made an appointment for me with the government officials in Dar-es-Salaam. He accompanied me in the call on the Tanganyika officers. Present in the meeting were the Chief Secretary (the equivalent of a prime minister), the Attorney General, and several staff people.

Dr. Anderson introduced me to the colonial officers in the meeting. I began by conveying greetings from Sir Andrew Cohen. It was clear that this immediately placed our conversation on a friendly level. I then announced that the Lutheran World Federation thought that enough time had elapsed since the war so that the German mission properties could be released.

The Chief Secretary reminded me that no peace treaty had yet been drawn up. From his point of view nothing could be done until such a time. I replied that we might then have to wait a long time. (A peace treaty has not been signed to this day). The Chief Secretary acknowledged this, but he countered with the possibility that if the properties were released, Russia might later insist that they should be used as war reparations.

I expressed surprise at the mention of reparations and inquired whether we were going to slip back from the high ground taken in the Versailles Treaty after World War I. (At Versailles the activity of Dr. J. H. Oldham, then the director of the International Missionary Council, secured the insertion of a special clause exempting all church and mission properties from being used for war reparations.) It was evident from the facial expression of the Chief Secretary that he was not aware of the Versailles Treaty's provision for exempting mission properties from confiscation, but I proceeded on the assumption that he recognized that a political precedent might exist. And so I ventured the conclusion that we could be reasonably certain that the United States would not take a lower ground now than the position taken at Versailles. To this I added that his government would most likely take a similar position.

The Chief Secretary granted this with a slight affirmative nod of the head. But he countered with the insistence that no one could be assured that Russia would support this position. I inquired whether he thought there was any risk if Great Britain and the United States stood together.

Quickly he interposed the warning that they could not allow the properties to be returned to the German mission societies. This provoked the Attorney General, a man of large stature, to slap the table with his fist, and literally shout, "Never, never, will we allow German missionaries back in Tanganyika!"

I listened to the Attorney General's speech but made no reply. I knew that from his point of view, there was adequate reason for his strong statement. In Dar-es-Salaam there is a peninsula that juts out into the beautiful harbor, where a German community hall had been built. It was a gathering place for German people in the area. At the front of the room a very large picture of Hitler had hung. For non-Germans it seemed to simulate an altar painting. When it was discovered by the British Government officers, it caused a deep-seated revulsion.

Here was a historical incident that looked like poison to some and at the same time was a symbol of hope to others. It must not be forgotten that Germany experienced a searing depression after World War I. (The Versailles Treaty played a part in this outcome.) The country was destitute and unemployment was staggering. Then in the early '30s the Nazis came to power under Hitler. Slowly the wheels of the German economy began to turn. Once more jobs were to be had. Many Americans who visited Germany in the mid-'30s pronounced Hitler as the "savior of Germany."

The missionaries working in Tanganyika had received many letters from home reporting the poverty of the people. And then suddenly improvement took place. The better times were associated with the name of Hitler. How could the missionaries think other than well of this "savior" of their nation? When the Nazis began to show themselves as the anti-Semitic tyranny they became, the information was slow in trickling out to Tanganyika. And then war broke out.

While some of these thoughts were chasing through my mind, I turned to the Chief Secretary and inquired, "If you cannot release the properties to the German mission societies, perhaps you could transfer them to the LWF—acting as a trustee for the churches. (The churches at that time were not incorporated and could not therefore qualify to hold land titles.) He replied with the cryptic question, "Are not the German churches members of the LWF?"

I countered with, "What about a transfer of the property to the USA Committee of the LWF? We would hold the properties in custody for and eventual transfer to the churches."

This proposal brought an affirmative reply. But now the Attorney General added a "safety provision." He said the legal instrument of transfer would place the properties in the name of Her Majesty, the Queen, and from Her Majesty's Government to the USA Committee. Thus there could be no transfer on the part of the USA Committee back to the German societies. Any effort to do this could bring immediate confrontation with Her Majesty's government.

The Chief Secretary indicated that some of the property would be retained for government purposes. But these properties would be paid for at approximate market prices.

When the transfer of monies took place, CYCOM made its decisions about their use in consultation with the German societies. In one of these decisions not only the German societies but also the Lutheran Church of Northern Tanganyika was consulted. This concerned a very desirable plantation property near Moshi called Makumira. It was set aside as a future location for the theological seminary. It was clear that Makumira would provide excellent acreage for the students to use for the support of themselves and their families.

The agreement consummated with the Tanganyika Colonial Government, serving under a mandate from the United Nations, was a great step forward. But there was also a depressing dimension. The Lund Assembly of the LWF had imposed a responsibility to confer with the German Mission Societies. How was the news of the property transaction to be broken to the German mission directors?

From the Tanganyika discussions I went directly to Germany. It was urgent to get there before the annual meeting of the German Evangelical Missionary Council would adjourn. The meetings were being held at the headquarters of the Neuendettelsau Mission Society in Bavaria.

A consultation was sought with the directors of the three societies concerned: Dr. D. S. Knak of the Berlin Society, Dr. Curt Ronicke of Bethel, and Dr. Carl Ihmels of Leipzig. Professor Walter Freytag, chairman of the Missionary Council, sat with us throughout the discussion. I faced this moment with some fear and trembling. Certainly, from the German point of view it could appear as though this young American pastor had maneuvered to transfer effective control of the Tanganyika properties to the American churches.

Before beginning my report I quietly prayed that God might use even the inflection of my voice to provide a proper understanding of what had transpired in the Dar-es-Salaam discussions with the Tanganyika government. When the report had been completed, I paused for their comment. There seemed to be little disposition to ask questions; only a few for some clarification. A heavy cloud of sorrow seemed to hang over the room. The time of waiting for some substantive comment seemed like an age, but I am sure it was no more than a few minutes. But then something happened. The senior among the four men was Dr. Knak. Slowly he rose to his feet. As he did so his right hand was preoccupied with playing with a watch chain stretched across his vest. My eyes could not help but scrutinize his suit. It was old and threadbare, likely from prewar days. His eyes were on the floor. Then he shifted his stance slightly and looked up, but all the while continuing to play with his watch chain.

Slowly his lips formed these words: "It is clear that we face a new day. And we must walk in God's new way."

I could have shouted, "Glory, hallelujah!" In this critical moment, when I am sure many emotions sought to take control of Dr. Knak's soul, he thrust aside cynicism and other negative attitudes. He willed to believe in what he discerned as Providence. It was evident that Dr. Knak had given voice to the judgment of his colleagues as well. The ground was cleared for counseling together about the work as a common task even though the effective decisions had to be made by CYCOM.

The consultations in Tanganyika were not only with missionary staff and government officers. It was also with indigenous African leaders. The most active of the several area churches was in northern Tanganyika, in the region of Mount Kilimanjaro. The church called itself the Evangelical Lutheran Church of Northern Tanganyika. At that time missionary Elmer Danielson was the president of the church and also superintendent of the missionary staff. The vice-president was a black pastor, the Rev. Lazarus Laiser.

Pastor Laiser was a gifted man but his formal education was limited. He knew that my visit to Tanganyika signaled a transfer of administration of the work from the Board of Foreign Missions of the Augustana Evangelical Lutheran Church to CYCOM of the USA Committee of the LWF. He wondered what lay back of this transfer. I explained it over and over again. But I could see that he was not satisfied. He knew what they had in the Augustana Board, but he was not sure that he could trust CYCOM. Suddenly he shot a question to me which I paraphrase, "What made you and your commission come out here for your announced purpose of helping us? You have not consulted with us."

I replied, "When your neighbor's house is on fire, you don't ask for permission to help extinguish the blaze. You provide help as quickly as possible. After the fire has been extinguished, you talk about relationships in any continuation of help that might be needed."

For the moment this seemed to satisfy him; but I could see there would be more questions coming. This probing attitude, mixed with a measure of wholesome suspicion, revealed a trust in the Augustana Board and Mr. Danielson, and a determination to be responsible for his church and his people in accepting a new relationship in the provision of overseas help. It was a friendly confrontation and it left us with a mutual respect for one another.

The churches in Tanganyika were calling for more missionaries. But the government had said *no* German missionaries would be allowed to come back. Informal conversations with Lutheran boards in the Scandinavian countries and in the U.S.A. revealed little disposition to call staff for Tanganyika unless they could be assured of tenure. If the government should change its policy in a few years and permit German missionaries to return, would this mean that other missionaries would have to pack up and go home?

To answer such a question and related issues it was necessary to call mission directors from the Scandinavian countries and the U.S.A. together for consultation with the German mission directors, the same four men to whom I had reported a few months earlier at Neuendettelsau. We now met in Stockholm in December 1949. It was explained to the German mission directors how difficult it would be to get properly trained youthful workers to accept a call if they thought that they might soon be replaced.

The German representatives recognized the necessity of providing the possibility of tenure for anyone who would be willing to go to Tanganyika in a missionary vocation. This mature attitude was expressed in a friendly spirit; but it was also obvious that there was an undertow of sorrow. Without a doubt they were nursing a quiet hope that something might happen to change the stringent policy action of the Tanganyika government.

Understanding and consensus had emerged from our discussions. But there was no readiness to break up the meeting. It seemed as though the Germans had something more to say. However, no one called for the floor. Then the silence was broken by Director Ronicke. He spoke up in a loud voice, "Who is it that says we cannot go back to work in Tanganyika?" For a few moments after this rhetorical question the silence was deafening. Then Director Ronicke's right arm shot upward, and he added, "It is Someone higher than we!" This vibrantly spoken confession of faith was followed by a soft voice announcing, "But I am sure that God will also have something for us Germans to do." Those of us who sat in that meeting felt we were on holy ground. Our consultation was ready to adjourn in a glow of God-given goodwill for one another.

Director Ronicke's words were prophetic. Within two years a German missionary who had been in Tanganyika before the war and who had special training for ministering to retarded people, was allowed to return. Not long thereafter selected medical missionaries were permitted to enter Tanganyika. And after a few years the missionary staff numbered American, Scandinavians, and Germans—all working together in concord.

In a visit to the theological seminary in Lawandai in the Usambara Mountain area, I was asked to speak to the students. Afterwards there were questions. One student by the name of Stefano Moshi persisted with questions. He followed me out of the building to the gate of the compound with one question after another.

As more and more African pastors were ordained, questions of church nomenclature came to the fore. Should a supervising pastor be called a president, a superintendent, a dean, or a bishop? Some strong opposition to the use of the term bishop was evident among American missionaries. European missionaries tended to favor its use. The African pastors who knew that the title bishop was in use among the Roman Catholics and the Anglicans made the sensible suggestion that some historical lectures be prepared. When this had been done and there had been opportunity for evaluation through discussion, the church approved the use of the title *bishop.* And each district area of Tanganyika became a diocese of the Evangelical Lutheran Church of Tanganyika. However, there was no authorization to address the presiding bishop as archbishop.

Ethiopia

One German mission society had been at work in Ethiopia; namely, the Hermannsburg Mission Society. In order to secure the release of their properties and permission to renew their missionary work, I had to seek an audience with his majesty, Emperor Haile Selassie.

The emperor was reputed to be a devout Christian man. A Swedish missionary told me that when Mussolini's army invaded Ethiopia, the emperor took up residence in London. On a visit in London during the war, the Swedish missionary called on the emperor. He was received with great warmth. After a short visit, the emperor said that he would like to bring his entire household together if the missionary would conduct a full worship service. He responded affirmatively. The congregation that assembled, from the emperor down to his servants, were attentive listeners and participants.

In seeking my audience with the emperor, I was a bit concerned about protocol. But friends were helpful. They told me that as soon as I entered the audience room I should bow formally. Then I was to advance half way toward the emperor and bow a second time. Thereafter I was to walk and bow a third time just before shaking hands with the emperor.

I found that I had been properly coached. As I sat down in an assigned chair, I made known the concern of the Hermannsburg Mission Society that its properties might be returned and permission granted to begin anew in their mission work. Without any hesitation the emperor said yes. He then turned to his secretary and instructed him to provide proper legal notification to the Hermannsburg Society.

This detail completed, the emperor initiated some conversation. He told me that when his reign began, it was almost impossible to get children to go to school. But now they had experienced an about-face. The government could not build schools fast enough to accommodate the children and youth who wanted an education.

The time for me to leave seemed to come very quickly. Protocol required walking backward to the door (one must not turn your back to the emperor). This backward walk was to be accompanied by three stops, with a bow to the emperor each time you paused.

There is an exceedingly important LWF project that is connected with Ethiopia. I refer to the Radio Voice of the Gospel (RVOG), the broadcasting station that was erected at Addis Ababa. The seed thought for the project was planted at the Commission on World Mission (CWM) annual meeting on Staten Island in the summer of 1957. Dr. Fridtjov Birkeli of Norway was at that time director of the LWF Department of World Mission. In giving his report he told about a visit in an African community where he was scheduled to speak. The group that had gathered to hear his address was smaller than he had anticipated. But after the meeting had adjourned, he saw a large group of people gathered in the marketplace listening to a "speaking box" (a portable radio). Dr. Birkeli commented, "I decided then, if people are so eager to hear the 'speaking box' maybe the church ought to consider what its responsibility is in such an age." He then proposed that the Department of World Mission should consider erecting a broadcasting station in Africa.

The proposal ignited considerable interest. Sigurd Aske, assistant to Dr. Birkeli, was asked to make a study of costs and feasibility, and report to the next annual meeting. At CWM's 1958 annual meeting in Sigtuna, Sweden, Aske's report revealed a project with heavy investment obligations. But he also made it clear that the cost estimates were dependable and manageable. After many questions and considerable discussion, the commission voted to recommend to the LWF's executive committee that the project be approved.

It was necessary to establish a place in Africa where the station might be located. All signs seemed to point to Addis Ababa in Ethiopia. The altitude in the city would allow beaming signals (broadcasts) to any part of Africa and to the entire Mid-East and on into parts of Asia. But one difficulty obtruded. The Near East Christian Council had already filed an application with the Ethiopian government for a franchise to broadcast. It seemed entirely out of order for two Christian organizations to be competing for the same privilege.

This situation required personal contact with the Near East Christian Council. We advised them of our intent. In the discussion that followed it was agreed that if the franchise should be awarded to them, they would constitute Party A and the LWF would be Party B. And if the LWF received the franchise, the Near East Christian Council would be Party B. Party A would be the owner and operator of the broadcasting station. Party B would be given special broadcast privileges at a preferred rental cost.

When the government made its decision, the franchise was given to the LWF. We learned later that the Archbishop of the Ethiopian Church was critical of the government's choice. We therefore decided that we would give the Ethiopian Church some broadcast time without charge. This pleased them.

CWM's recommendation to the LWF Executive Committee was placed before them at an annual meeting in Strasbourg, France. During the discussion, Dr. Fry, president of the LWF, objected to building a broadcasting station in Ethiopia. He pointed out that if a coup should take place and the emperor should be overthrown, we could easily lose our entire investment in a matter of days or in a few weeks. This put a damper on the enthusiasm. There was little forthright discussion but a lot of frustration noises. Then Bishop Hanns Lilje called for the floor. He spoke soberly and deliberately in saying, "If we are going to wait until we are sure that our money will not be lost, or certain that the investment will pay off, then the church will never get anything done."

After this comment a call for the vote was sounded. The question was put, and passed by a decisive voice vote. My recollection is that it was unanimous. As that session adjourned, Professor Tiililä, the Church of Finland's representative on the executive committee, rose and said, "This authorization for the erection of the broadcasting station in Ethiopia is the most important decision we have made in the many years in which I have served on this body."

February 26, 1963, the station was dedicated with the name Radio Voice of the Gospel (RVOG). The daily broadcasts aired carefully edited newscasts as well as worship services and Bible study. I recall an Arab cab driver in Egypt told me that when they heard newscasts from Moscow or Peking, they always compared them with what came from RVOG. That determined for them where the truth lay.

I cannot leave this segment on Ethiopia without calling attention to the stalwart Christian laymen in this church. Some of them were well-educated, thoroughly versed in the Christian faith. And no one had to wonder where their commitments were. Witness was by word and deed.

Palestine

Five German mission societies have been at work in Palestine since the turn of the century. They cooperated under the name of Palestinawerk.

These societies served in elementary school education in vocational training. They ministered through medical work and evangelism. Arabs were attracted to espouse the Christian faith in sufficient numbers so that Christian Arab congregations came into being in Jerusalem, Bethlehem, Beit Jala, Ramallah, and in Jaffa on the coast.

Jews were almost nonexistent in Palestine until the Zionist movement was organized in the last part of the last century. Under its promotion Jews began to move back to the land of their fathers. The Zionists purchased land from rich Arab landowners and settled the Jewish emigrants on the land. In 1922, 11% of a Palestinian population of 757,000 were Jews. In 1929 the Jews had increased to 16% of a total population of 900,000.

The land that was sold to the Zionists for Jewish use had been tilled by Arab peasants. Although they had been renters only, their families had lived on the same piece of land for generations. They therefore carried a proprietary feeling for the land . . . even though they had been renters only.

When the owner sold the land, the peasant Arab renters were evicted. There was then no place to go, and so they became rootless refugees. In 1953 the director of the United Nations Relief and Works Administration reported that there were 868,350 Arab refugees. Most of these were in camps on the West Bank.

The United Nations ministered to physical needs of the refugees; but the limited substance of this ministry left many marginal areas of need. Church organizations tried to provide supplemental care. Among these none provided more help than Lutheran World Relief (LWR). From 1948 to 1954 LWR distributed 7,017,468 pounds of clothing and other relief goods valued at $2,503,500. Assistance of this kind was provided almost continuously until the present time.

In the late '60s I had an experience that revealed how strongly this ministry had registered in the minds of the Arabs. Dr. Edwin Moll, a pastor of the United Lutheran Church, had been in charge of CYCOM's service to the refugees and the assistance that we provided the Palestinawerk activities. I had been conducting discussions with the Government of Israel for the release of German mission properties in Israel. It was necessary for me to go to the Jordanian side to meet with Dr. Moll and his staff to ascertain what their budget needs would be for the ensuing year.

Jerusalem at that time was a divided city, the eastern part in the hands of King Hussein and his government, and the western part was governed by Israel. Anyone passing from one part of the city to the other had to go through what was called the Mandelbaum Gate. Both sides of the gate were under the strict surveilance of a military police force. I now had to present myself at this gate.

I was peremptorily challenged by the Arab guard. A second guard looked over the shoulder of the first one as he was examining my papers. Suddenly he exclaimed, "This man is with the LWF; we *must* allow him to pass through."

My identification with the LWF and the LWR gave me immediate carte blanche privileges. Why? Because of all that LWR had done for the homeless Arab refugees. In the moment of that experience I wished that all of our supporting people at home could have observed what their gifts had done in an area that was otherwise ruled by hate.

The mission property issues that claimed CYCOM's attention and help in other parts of the world were also very real in Palestine. Israel had confiscated a number of Palestinawerk properties that were located within Israeli boundaries. The situation was loaded with sensitivities. And so we made approaches at several different levels.

Dr. Moll was involved as was Dr. S. C. Michelfelder, then the General Secretary of the LWF. He coopted the help of a Swiss lawyer, Dr. Max Habicht—and also Dr. Fred Nolde, director of the Commission of Churches on International Affairs of the World Council of Churches. The mention of Nolde's name compels me to pause for an observation. He was a theological professor on leave from the faculty at Mt. Airy Seminary in Philadelphia. Much of his work kept him at the meetings of the United Nations in Geneva. Few people were known as well and as favorably among UN representatives as Fred Nolde. To walk with him through the UN corridors was to see him greeted by one delegate after another. And it seemed as though he was on a first name basis with all of them. Fred Nolde's sources of information made him a dependable consultant for CYCOM in all international legal matters. And this was also true as we addressed ourselves to the Palestinawerk property matters in Israel.

The Israeli government man who was our main contact was Mr. Haim Kadmon of their Department of Justice. In mid-May 1951 Dr. Michelfelder summoned me to Geneva because Mr. Kadmon was ready to begin discussions about the Palestinawerk properties. We had about 12 different sessions in our discussions. The minutes of the CYCOM meeting September 26, 1951, record this important beginning: "Our point of reference in seeking a settlement was the agreement that whatever settlement might be made must provide the basis of goodwill in the constituencies of the two negotiating parties."

We arrived at an outline for an agreement that we wanted to check with Palestinawerk. This we did and three months later—in August—Mr. Kadmon was back in Geneva. Dr. Fry, as president of the LWF was also in Geneva for a meeting of the Executive Committee. The two men signed the official agreement on behalf of Israel and the LWF for Palestinawerk.

The agreement provided title for the church compounds in Haifa and Tel Aviv. On 13 other properties the LWF waived rights to the ownership in exchange for monetary compensation by the government of Israel. The compensation was to be $50,000 of US money and 550,000 Israeli pounds. The Israeli money was to be paid in three installments over a period of nine years.

But even after the agreement was signed much work remained to be done. This was occasioned by the problem of exchange. Palestinawerk wanted to use the property compensation of 550,000 pounds for continuing their work among the Arabs. And since this would be on the West Bank, which at that time was a part of the Kingdom of Jordan, the money would have to be exchanged for Jordanian dinars.

But how could this be accomplished? The Israeli pound was originally intended to carry a value comparable to the British sterling; namely, about $2.80 per pound. However, the Israeli currency was so weak that if you took it out of Israel to the international exchange market, a pound would produce no more than 35 cents. This was impossible. We weighed the possibility of using the indemnity money in Israel for the purchase of merchandise that might be sold abroad. But the expense would have wasted any gains that might have been realized. Help was forthcoming from another source.

About this time Prime Minister Adenauer of Germany announced a sizable sum of German marks to compensate Israel and Israeli citizens for losses they had incurred in Germany. That suggested a possibility. If we could pay the Israeli indemnity funds back to the Israeli government in exchange for an equivalent value in their assignment of the strong German marks, Palestinawerk could use them for their work in Jordan.

This possibility was explored with Mr. Kadmon, and he was willing to check it out. In this process the Israeli Finance Ministry and the Bonn government had to be contacted. Both governments referred us to the two special commissions (one for Germany and one for Israel) that were handling the indemnity money payments. We were notified that there would be a joint meeting of the two commissions at the Hague in Holland. The proper thing would be to place the matter before them.

And so I made a special trip to the Hague. The two commissions approved our proposal and notified their respective governments accordingly. The use of this exchange arrangement resulted in each Israeli pound producing the equivalent of $1.65 in purchasing Jordanian dinars. This was something far different than 35 cents for each pound. The entire transaction moved along so smoothly that we had to acknowledge that the Lord of the Church had walked before us in our contacts and discussions. But I must also point out that the Israeli government seemed very pleased in the knowledge that the money would be used for a ministry among the Arab refugees.

I find it appropriate to conclude this segment on Palestine with a World Council of Churches' prayer release:

> Almighty God, whose blessed Son had no place on earth to lay His head, we thank Thee with all our hearts that, having kept us from the tribulations which many of Thy children suffer, Thou has permitted us to dwell peacefully in the land that we love.
>
> Open our hearts to the sorrows of the refugees, who, through the cruelty of men and for the sake of that which they believed, have suffered the loss of those good things which we enjoy, and now live as aliens and outcasts, having nothing that they can call their own.
>
> Help us to remember that it is not for our merits, but only of Thy grace that we have been preserved.
>
> Inspire our nation to take courageous and generous action for the sake of the refugees. And make Thy Church a place in which the homeless find a home, the hopeless recover hope, and the wounds of men are healed, through the love of Thy only Son, our Savior, Jesus Christ. Amen.

Indonesia

Indonesia comprises the islands called the Dutch East Indies before World War II. Holland ruled as a colonial power until World War II broke out. Japan invaded and became the new colonial power. But the fortunes of war changed and Japan retreated from the Dutch East Indies. That became the occasion for the Indonesians to assert themselves and to set up the Republic of Indonesia. The Dutch returned and tried to impose their former colonial administration. They succeeded in part, particularly in metropolitan centers. All of this intensified the feelings of antipathy toward the nations of the Occident.

One of the large and vigorous tribal groupings in Indonesia is the Batak people. They live largely in central Sumatra with a considerable spill-over in Java. The Bataks were largely animists and were suspicious of foreigners. Two American churches became concerned about them and planned to send out missionaries. The first missionary to arrive was killed. When the second church sent its missionary representative, he too suffered martyrdom.

In 1861 Ludwig I. Nommensen of Denmark was sent to Sumatra by the Rhenish Missionary Society of Barmen in the Rhineland. Nommensen knew what had happened to the Americans. He proceeded with care but also with resolute courage. His first testing came as he pitched a tent house on a hill overlooking a large marketplace. During the night someone tried to collapse his tent. The would-be attackers were too noisy and Nommensen was alerted in time to escape.

The next morning the tall stalwart Nommensen strode down into the center of the marketplace. He got the attention of the people and called out, "The gods you worship take life; the God whom I worship gives life. It is he whom I have come to proclaim." Thereafter he began a life of proclamation, teaching, and baptizing. By the time he died in 1918 there were 180,000

Christians among the Bataks. In 1952 there were 740,000 Christians. Today the Batak church membership is over a million baptized Christians.

The church is known by its Batak name, *Huria Kristen Batak Protestant,* or simply by its initials HKBP. The church was represented at the constituting assembly of the World Council of Churches in Amsterdam, Holland, in 1948. The International Missionary Council knew that the war years had destroyed many things for the Bataks, and that they needed help. In conversation with the Batak delegates, they could get no information about what their needs might be. The Bataks were not about to admit need of any kind while on Dutch soil; it would seem like an admission that the new republic could not manage in its own household. The IMC thereupon turned to the LWF and said, "You Lutherans better see what you can do."

Bishop Johannes Sandegren of the Tamil Evangelical Lutheran Church in south India had initiated a personal fact-finding mission through a visit to Indonesia in the spring of 1947. He proceeded with great care. He understood very well the intensity of feelings the Indonesians harbored against the Dutch. And often these feelings were directed toward all white people.

Bishop Sandegren traveled to the capitol city of Djakarta, known as Tatavia among the Dutch. There he was informed that it would be impossible to get into the interior of Sumatra, where most of the Batak congregations were located. It was also reported that the Bataks would not receive a white man.

On the way home, God gave Bishop Sandegren the impulse to seek out an Indian to visit the Batak church. If a white man was not welcome, perhaps a brown or a black man would be. And maybe it would be well to send a doctor of medicine instead of a pastor. This impulse came with such force that it seemed to carry its own authority.

In the Tamil church there was an upstanding wise Christian layman who was also a doctor of medicine. Bishop Sandegren arranged for this layman, Dr. Williams, to go to Sumatra in November 1947. Wisely, he sought and obtained permission to ride on a United Nations plane into central Sumatra, arriving there in March 1948. The Bataks received him warmly. He had not been there long before the Ephorus (the title for the head of the church) evaluated his work with the words, "Dr. Williams has been a doctor for the spirit as well as a doctor for the body."

Through Dr. Williams' ministry, Bishop Sandegren was given an official invitation to visit the HKBP. Before accepting he insisted that the LWF should send a younger American pastor to accompany him. And so it happened that Bishop Sandegren and I went to Indonesia in November 1948.

The United Nations had stepped in to arrange a truce between the Dutch and the Republic. To pass from one area into the other required a military pass from both the Dutch and the Republican military authorities. We began by traveling to Medan, Sumatra, an area under the Dutch government, but also a point of departure for the interior of Sumatra.

In Medan we lived with a Dutch missionary named Bos and his family. Missionary Bos was very helpful in obtaining for us the two required military passes. But we were warned that there was considerable guerrilla activity in the border area and we were not to proceed until the authorities approved.

After a week of waiting the Dutch military office in Medan telephoned that we might proceed the next morning. However, we were cautioned to stop at Siantar, a city near the border. There we were to consult with the Dutch army post's military intelligence officer.

In Siantar we put up at a motel and then visited the army post's office. There we were advised not to go in. They added that they would not take our military pass away from us; but if we decided to use it, we must remember that it was strictly at our own risk.

At the motel Bishop Sandegren told me that I would have to

make the decision. He explained that he had lived a full life (he was about 70 years of age at that time), and so it would not matter too much if something should happen to him. But "you," he said, "have reason to believe that you may have many more years in which to work."

What a position to be in! A younger person never likes to make a decision that would govern the actions of a respected colleague who is his senior by many years. But there was no mistaking that Bishop Sandegren meant what he said.

I was silent for a long time. There seemed to be a battery of voices speaking within my mind. But after a while, it settled down to two thoughts. One was represented by Jesus' word to Satan during the wilderness temptation: "It is said 'you shall not tempt the Lord your God' " (Luke 4:12). The second thought that vied for attention was Jesus' word to men whom he encountered along the road who wanted time to turn aside before responding to his call. Jesus replied, "No one who puts his hand to the plow and looks back is fit for the kingdom of God" (Luke 9:62).

Was there a word from God in one of these two Bible passages? Would we be tempting God if we went farther into Sumatra against the counsel of the Dutch intelligence officer? After all, there was no purpose in going just to prove that we were courageous. But then Jesus' word about turning back after the hand had been put to the plow asserted itself. The civil war in my mind was finally resolved by the second word, and peace followed immediately. I looked up at Bishop Sandegren and said, "We are going in."

A smile that I can still see spread across Bishop Sandegren's face and he replied, "Very well." We reported our decision to the military and asked them to send word to the Batak Ephorus at the church office in Balige in the interior.

Early the next morning we moved on. We reached the United Nations status quo line just before noon. Before us stood the

Ephorus with his entire church council to bid us welcome. When the proper exchange of greetings had been made, the Ephorus gathered us in a circle and led us in the singing of:

Abide in grace, Lord Jesus,
Among us constantly,
Lest Satan's art deceive us
And gain the victory.

Several stanzas were sung and then the Ephorus called upon Bishop Sandegren to lead in prayer. This prayer followed:

O God, our God, a mighty fortress and a trusty shield and weapon, a help for those that seek thee and a succor for those that place their trust in thee.

To thee, our God, we give thanks for thou hast brought us to this meeting at the boundary between the two states. Thou hast led us together here in peace and concord. In thy hands we are safe, under thy protection we go secure. Now we pray thee to guide us still in all our ways, to prosper our outgoing and incoming, to bless the enterprise which in thy name we have taken in hand, and let us achieve the purpose for which we meet now on the borderline.

So shall the task end to the welfare of thy people and to the glory of thy holy name. To thee be praise now and forever. Amen.

As we lifted our bowed heads, we noted that frontier guards from both the Dutch and Republican forces had been a part of our circle of worshipers. In Christ friends and "enemies" become one.

Late that afternoon an official reception was given us at Balige. A dinner was served us in the parish house adjoining the church. Members of the Batak Church Council, pastors, and some government officials were present; and colorfully garbed Batak women served. In the official statement of welcome the Ephorus told us that ever since he had dispatched the letter of invitation, the Batak congregations had been praying for our safety. In that moment I breathed a prayer of thanksgiving that the Lord of the Church had stayed our feet from turning around when the Dutch intelligence service advised us against going into the Republican territory.

A meeting with the church council followed the evening meal. Questions of need, missionary help that might be desired, and their inquiry about membership in the LWF were discussed. Copies of important articles in the LWF constitution were read and distributed for their information. We cautioned them against making an immediate decision in filing an application for membership. Rather, would it not be well for them to place the matter before each of their eight district conventions? If after such a democratic procedure, they were still convinced that they wished to join the LWF, the application might be presented by the Ephorus at the next LWF assembly. This very soft sell was a conscious choice. There were some voices in the world that were ready to accuse the LWF of "capturing the Batak Church." And therefore we were doubly careful that the Bataks should be sure about what they wanted. We wanted that everything that was done should be in the full view of all interested parties.

In a report by the Ephorus our hearts were gladdened by the information that the civil war had not dampened their concern for evangelism. The church was continuing to grow despite the difficult times.

After our meeting with the church council the Ephorus showed us a schedule of several days of visitation among the congregations. In each place the church was packed with people; even standing room was preempted. And both Bishop Sandegren and I had to speak at each stop. Their interest and concentrated attention was eloquently demonstrated by the actions of a 12-year-old boy. He could not get into the church and so he crawled up the outside church wall so that he could hook his elbows in the sill of an open window. Before long a man sitting in a pew below the window spotted him. He took his umbrella and struck the boy on the head. Immediately the boy disappeared, but not for long. He must have found something on the outside that he could stand on. With his eyes barely even with the window sill, he continued to look in and to listen. But now he could not be seen by the man with the umbrella.

When our automobile rolled over the country roads and through the villages, children swarmed to the roadside and saluted with bright smiles and the nationalist greeting *Merdeka,* their word for freedom and independence. In the two largest centers on our itinerary we found that church council members and community government officials were often the same people. Wherever we went among their congregations, invariably we would find the picture of the pioneer missionary Nommensen. This strong servant of Christ had laid foundations that supported the early emergence of the autonomous Batak church.

The time for our leaving came all too soon. It was with considerable reluctance that we took leave of the Ephorus, associated Batak leaders, and Dr. Williams on the morning of November 18. Once more we paused at the United Nations status quo line for a brief period of worship under the leadership of the Ephorus. We had not only made the acquaintance of the Batak church leaders and their people, but we had also come to revere and love them.

When I returned to New York, my first day at the office in what was then the ULCA Church House, I encountered Dr. Fry the moment I entered the building. He stepped toward me with outstretched arms and hugged me much as my father would do when I was a child. The news that had reached New York reported that Bishop Sandegren and I had entered the interior of Sumatra against the government's advice. And so Dr. Fry, chairman of CYCOM, seemed to regard my return as an emergence from the valley of the shadow of death.

When I entered my office and looked at the mail on the top of my desk, a cablegram caught my immediate attention. It was an application from the HKBP for membership in the LWF. We had cautioned them to wait until they could get the reaction of their church in the eight district conventions that were soon to meet. But their church council was evidently sure enough of the thinking of their people to feel that no waiting was required. The application was approved by the LWF Executive Committee in the summer of 1949.

New Guinea

In 1950 I invested January 31 and all of February in New Guinea.

The Neuendettelsau and Rhenish Mission Societies of Germany pioneered work in New Guinea. During and after World War I, the former Iowa Synod administered the work of these two societies. In 1925 the United Evangelical Lutheran Church of Australia joined with the Iowa Synod to assist in the work. The two German societies returned to the field in 1930. The Iowa Synod thereupon accepted an assignment in the Finnesterre mountains, lying between the fields of the two societies. In 1943 the Rhenish Mission withdrew and relinquished its so-called Madang field to the Iowa Synod. That same year the Neuendettelsau Mission Society insisted on splitting the field which had been operated as one united mission field since the war years. This divided arrangement was completed in 1933 and continued until World War II.

When war conditions permitted a return of missionaries, the work on the Madang field of the former American Lutheran Church and on the Finschhafen field of the Neuendettelsau Society was once more operated as a joint venture administered by the Board of Foreign Missions of the American Lutheran Church. The United Evangelical Lutheran Church in America made a substantial contribution of personnel and assumed a small part of the budget.

The coastal line of the two mission fields adds up to between 250 and 300 miles. The mission field extends inland from 50 to 75 miles. Rugged mountain ranges extend along the coast, covered everywhere with dense jungle growths. Back some 50 miles from the coast in what is known as the Central highland, there are open plateau valleys with larger population groups than one finds at the coast. The mission's statistical committee estimated that there were 119,294 people on the Madang field with 18,013 Christians, and 283,243 people on the Finschhafen field, with a Christian population of 76,714. This made a total Christian community of 94,727.

My first 12 days in New Guinea were used to sit with the missionaries in their annual conference. Their sessions were held in the forenoon, afternoon, and evening. Only once did the conference set aside an afternoon for recreation. Despite the protracted sessions, humidity, and heat, the missionaries attended sessions faithfully and participated in floor discussions with great vigor. That year's conference became historic in the fact that it was the first time that representative Papuan elders had been invited to sit with the conference.

The missionaries were a bit fearful that one of the European societies might, as was done after World War I, request that the united administration of the work be discontinued. Unitedly, they adopted a resolution asking that this be avoided at all costs. Evidently the Papuan elders who were sitting with the conference caught this concern. While the conference was still in session, two Papuan schoolteachers composed a letter about it and delivered it to me. It was a bit awkwardly stated, but there is no mistaking the spirit in which they wrote, and their conviction that their point of view had been garnered from the Bible.

There were postwar property problems in New Guinea as there were in other areas where CYCOM carried responsibilities. However, since the former American Lutheran Church had been asked by the German societies to care for their work, this had been done. Dr. T. P. Fricke, executive director of the Board of Foreign Missions of the American Lutheran Church, met with the government of Australia in Canberra. The government agreed to recognize Dr. Fricke's board as the supervising agent for the united work. And Dr. Fricke was ably assisted by Dr. John Kuder, the field superintendent.

New Guinea work dealt with people who lived a very primitive life. The most backward areas were designated by the government as "controlled areas." In such locations there could be people who practiced cannibalism. But no one was allowed to go into the uncontrolled areas without a government permit.

The Papuans were only a jump away from the stone age. But they responded to education. There was no mistaking their abilities. And they did not find the gospel difficult to grasp. To ascertain this I conducted an impromptu test one Sunday morning. The result of that test is one of my fondest memories of the visit in New Guinea.

The test was given in a congregation on Mt. Sattelberg. I knew Dr. Kuder expected me to preach. But as we walked up the road to the church, I suddenly became aware that I did not know what went on in the minds of the people whom I had encountered. If I was always going to do the speaking when I appeared before a congregation, there wasn't much likelihood of really getting to know the Christian conviction of these Papuans. And so I decided I would catechize the people instead of preaching a sermon. But I said nothing to Dr. Kuder about my decision—lest he would put up a vigorous protest.

When the service progressed to the time for the sermon, I began by telling them, "I noticed that when Pastor Kuder and I arrived many of you were standing in small groups visiting with one another outside the church building. Some of you spoke with enough animation that I could hear your words. But since I do not understand your language, I do not know what you were saying to one another. I noted that at times you used the word *Jesus.* When you did this, your facial expression reflected respect, joy, and love. Why do you love this Jesus?"

Before I could call on anyone to answer, a man sitting on a front bench got up and said, "It is easy to answer your question. Before the missionaries came to us, we lived a life of fear. For us it seemed as though evil spirits were everywhere: in the woods, in the water, the grass, and in the stones. If we built a new house for ourselves, and someone said that an evil spirit had moved into the house, we would not dare to spend the night in it.

"Then the missionaries came to us. They taught us about God, and about Jesus. And when we opened our lives to him, our fears disappeared." And then he beamed, "That's why we love Jesus!" I could see that the people in the congregation supported his witness.

It was worth going to New Guinea to hear this Papuan Christian proclaim his love for the Jesus whose presence displaces fear.

China

In the summer of 1948 when I was facing the decision about the Executive Secretaryship of CYCOM, a college classmate, Daniel Nelson, who had become a recognized missionary statesman, insisted that I must accept the call. To have his endorsement made it easier to say yes.

Daniel Nelson was born in China of pioneer missionary parents. He came to the United States for his advanced education. This was done solely that he might be equipped to return to China to serve a people whom he loved with heart and mind. He became an intrepid and innovative missionary in a time of great disturbance in the national life of China. He was ordained in 1928 and served in China during 1928-34; 1935-41; 1944-48.

Dan was the first Lutheran missionary to bring an automobile with him to help in covering the large area in the province of

Honan where he was responsible. The way in which he passed the custom's inspection tells a lot about Dan's spirit and his attitude to the Chinese. When he announced himself with the car, the busy customs inspector brushed him aside with the words, "I am too busy to look at your car now. You will have to wait."

Dan was not the typical westerner expecting to be given preferred attention. He responded, "I know that you are a very busy man. I have lots of time (a euphemism); I can wait." And so he sat down on a nearby bench and relaxed.

It was not too long before the customs man courteously advised him that he would now look at the car. The inspection was quickly completed and the necessary papers were drawn. This done, the inspector was about to turn to another customer, when Dan exclaimed, "Oh, I forgot! I have a second car." The customs man was about to blow a gasket; and then Dan took out of his pocket a rubber toy car that he was bringing home for his son. When the government man saw it, he relaxed in laughter. He loved this informal and friendly American.

On two furlough periods to the USA, Dan had done extensive graduate work in Chinese studies. This formal acquaintance with the Chinese people, added to his years of living among them, made him one of the most knowledgeable Lutheran missionaries in China. His obvious dedication to the will of his Lord, plus a great capacity to discern hope in every difficult situation, made Dan a marked man.

Dr. Ralph Long, the General Secretary of the National Lutheran Council and of the USA Committee of the Lutheran World Federation, asked Dan to assume responsibility for the "orphaned missionaries" in China. In the years of 1944-48 Dan was referred to under the designation, Director of the LWF in China. A small group of selected missionaries were asked to serve as Dr. Nelson's advisory committee.

This was a rocky period when the Communists were seizing power in many parts of north and central China, and marauding robber bands were also active in central China. And the invasion of the Japanese made large parts of the country a war zone. After Pearl Harbor the missionaries either evacuated to west China or were interned by the Japanese.

Under Dan Nelson's forceful direction—in consultation with his friend, Dr. Peng-fu, the Chinese president of the Lutheran Church of China, a number of distinctive projects were carried out:

1) A Lutheran headquarters office was set up in Chungking in western China. From there Dr. Nelson disbursed orphaned missions assistance to German and Scandinavian missionaries.

2) The theological seminary was moved from Shekow, near Hankow, to Chungking. In a few years it was moved back to Shekow. But the pressures of the Peking government limited the seminary's work. Once again it moved, this time to Hong Kong. There it has continued to prepare pastors and lay workers for the churches in Hong Kong, Taiwan, Borneo, and Malaya.

3) A Lutheran Mission Center was located in Shanghai through the lease of a China Inland Mission building. This became a mission hostel for missionaries who were leaving the country. It also served as an interim home for a few newly-arrived missionaries who came to help out in some of the orphaned mission areas.

4) The unsettled conditions made it extremely difficult to travel, and worse yet, to make proper distribution of the physical necessities for life. In this situation Dan Nelson bought a DC-3 airplane in 1946. He organized a crew and put the plane into service for Lutheran missions and for others. He named the plane St. Paul. A second DC-3 was bought to provide parts for repair work on the St. Paul when this was needed. The plane flew into many parts of China. Only God knows how many lives were saved by this innovative service.

Dan Nelson's schedule was an enervating one. To recoup

strength and to have a little time with his family, Dan planned a week of vacation on the Portuguese Island of Macao in July 1948. Refreshed, and on their way to Hong Kong July 16, the plane crashed and the entire family lost their lives.

What a sacrifice the Nelson family had to make! The senior Daniel Nelson, a pioneer Lutheran missionary to China, was shot by bandits February 8, 1926, at 73 years of age. An older son, Bert, lost his life while he was a captive of a robber band in Honan during December 1934. And now, the youngest son, Daniel Jr., was drowned with his family in an airplane accident off the coast of south China. On September 25, 1948, a Nelson memorial service was conducted for relatives and friends in Central Lutheran Church, Minneapolis.

CYCOM authorized the appointment of the Rev. Arthur Olson as Dan Nelson's successor. He had been Dan's dependable helper, and like him, was a China missionary of many years' experience.

My visit to China in CYCOM's service was during October 14-November 1; and November 25-December 17 in 1949. At a meeting of CYCOM's Commission before I left, we had before us a request for a salary increase for the St. Paul's three member crew: the pilot, assistant pilot, and the engineer. The crew was being paid on a commercial salary scale. And the commission, accustomed to dealing with missionary salary levels, felt the crew was well paid. They were therefore reluctant to grant their request. However, they made no decision but asked me to discuss it with the crew.

This I did. I explained the feeling of the commission and the crew members listened carefully. Without any resentment in his voice, the pilot answered on behalf of the crew. And this was his reply: "If you will give us a call like that which you give your missionaries, we will fly the St. Paul for a missionary's salary." The pilot pointed to a factor that those of us who serve the church may often overlook. Most of the time there is an element of security in the church's service, that many other workers do not have.

In early 1950 the need for the services of the St. Paul was far less pressing than in early 1949. Operation was therefore discontinued March 20, 1950. By authorization of the commission, the plane was sold at a very reasonable price to Captain Dudding, the pilot, and to his engineer, Max Springweiler. They looked forward to using the plane for ad hoc commercial needs. A severance pay was granted to the entire crew. This was voted at the going rate of the two larger commercial airlines operating in China. Both CYCOM, the China advisory committee, and the crew parted company with mutual feelings of respect and appreciation.

Pastor Olson had arranged before I arrived to have a meeting of all Protestant mission leaders in Hong Kong for tea shortly after I landed at the airport. About 20 people were present. Most of them were China mission superintendents or missionaries waiting to get into China. In two hours of questions and discussion a number of facts were gleaned about what the church was facing under the Peking government. There was also opportunity to talk with Dr. Peng-fu, president of the Lutheran Church of China. He had recently come from the interior. With Dr. Peng-fu was Mr. C. H. Chen, editor of *Hsin I Pao,* the Lutheran Church's fortnightly paper. Mr. Chen had just arrived from Hankow.

There are so many reports that have come to the West from the Communist China of over 25 years ago, that I shall not mention more than a few impressions that linger. Reports of church life varied in different places. Most of the churches of the Norwegian Mission Society had been closed and continued to be closed at the time of my visit. From practically all centers came stories of some defections in the Christian congregations. But there were also a number of stories of deepening faith, good church attendance, and seekers who would join with small private fellowship groups. A number of such small groups were active among students.

At a brief meeting of the board of the Lutheran Church in China, Dr. Hjalmar Swanson (the Board Secretary of the Augustana Lutheran Church of that day) and I were asked by President Peng-fu to bring the following word to the Lutheran mission leaders in the USA:

"Retain a skeletal staff in Hong Kong. We need such a staff in order to maintain contacts.

"Do not discontinue your sacrificial gifts of love and support. Tell the church in America that the work is still going forward; the work in China has a future. There is a danger that people in America may think that the missionaries in Hong Kong are idle; but they are active. There are seven new places in the colony where services are conducted at least twice each Sunday. The time is coming when missionaries should be returned to China.

"We greet our American brethren in the words of Psalm 24."

The same needs that required the provision of a Lutheran Center in Shanghai made it necessary to provide a center in Hong Kong. The British Crown Colony would allow no travelers to enter Hong Kong unless they had an assured address where they might stay. The need was so evident that I cabled New York for permission to buy property in consultation with the advisory committee. There was an immediate reply from New York. And so we bought a very serviceable building at a cost of $70,000. It is located at 33 Granville Road, and it has served well as a center and a missionary home. The property was registered in the name of the advisory committee to begin with, but on August 7, 1951, LWF ownership was recorded in the government office. In turning aside from the visit in China, it should be reported that CYCOM sought to help the orphaned mission work by its financial policies as well as by the actual gifts. All budgets governing the assistance that was given were computed in the currency of the nation in which a church was located. Because the American dollar was strong at that time the exchange rate was always in our favor. By reckoning the budget of a church to be helped in the currency of its own nation, the value of Lutheran World Action gifts was multiplied. This resulted in more churches being assisted than what would otherwise have been possible.

Sometimes there would be church officers that would ask to get the gift in dollars. This happened in a meeting with the Batak church council in Indonesia. I explained that this was against our policy. By handling the exchange ourselves we were able to help more needy churches. My reply did not seem to make a dent in the man who had asked the question. He responded with the cryptic statement, "Do you mean to say that if you give me a sheep, and the sheep has a lamb, you are going to take the lamb away from me?"

Exchange help was also provided in another manner. The British pound sterling was worth $2.80 in the international money exchanges. The governments of European countries found British sterling much easier to use in funding foreign obligation—dollars were just too expensive. It therefore became very costly for European mission societies to obtain dollars for use in dollar areas of the world.

In this situation we sold dollars to the mission societies of Europe in exchange for their sterling at the normal price of $2.80. And since many of the churches we assisted were located in sterling areas, we could use the English currency without any loss. And our brethren in the European societies could send their money abroad without suffering a debilitating discount.

I conclude this chapter with one of many expressions of gratitude that CYCOM received from those who were on the receiving end of orphaned missions activity. The witness is from one of the most erudite of mission leaders in the war and postwar period, Professor Walter Freytag, general secretary of the German Missionary Council: "Immeasurable has been the spiritual effect of orphaned mission aid. Both the younger churches abroad and the church in Germany experienced the unity of Christendom in the midst of great trouble. During the period of the Third Reich the German churches were strengthened in their struggle by this aid. In the misery of the postwar period it served as a sign of hope. Today it is our impulse to make every possible effort to again assume our task—and at the same time it is an exhortation to comprehend our services as our share in the service of the entire Christendom.

"We thank all those who have made such great sacrifices for us. They are for us the hands of God, which have held us and are now guiding us on to new service, toward his goal."

5

BEYOND RACE

BOTH WORLD WAR I AND WORLD WAR II shook American people in many different ways. Population movements brought many rural citizens into the big cities. The easy availability of automobile transportation sent people moving into other states and often into a completely different region in the nation. The military draft homogenized the youth of the nation. In the process new ideas and culture patterns were felt throughout the country.

The race issue asserted itself in the south by many forms of discrimination. In the north there tended to be not a little of smugness; hadn't the north gone to war to free the slaves? But this self-righteousness soon began to disappear; in its place varying degrees of discrimination found acceptance. I remember while teaching summer school in northern Wisconsin, I was visiting with my host one evening (the practice was for the parochial school teacher to be hosted by a different family each week). The conversation drifted into the area of race relations. Suddenly my host turned to me and inquired, "Do you really think God has given the black man a soul?"

It was easy to remind him that if I didn't believe that God had created all races with a soul, I would not be planning to be a foreign missionary. I then launched a little Bible study through conversation.

After I had retired to my room that evening I asked myself, "How did this Norwegian immigrant member of a Lutheran congregation come up with a subtle racial discrimination such as his question revealed?" Certainly he did not bring it with him from Norway. Had we failed our people by not relating biblical truth to social issues of the day?

From my understanding of the New Testament I could find no room for harboring any prejudice against black people. This position had been strongly fortified by my associations in the Student Volunteer Movement for Foreign Missions and in the Lutheran Student Association of America. Christian student movements were alert to nail racial discrimination as a sin.

In my third year at St. Olaf, the college was awarded a chapter of Pi Kappa Delta, a national honor forensic society. All who had represented the college in oratory or debate that year were eligible for charter membership in the chapter. Not until a year later did it become known that Pi Kappa Delta admitted only Caucasian students. I wrote to the national office to protest the policy. I received a courteous answer, advising me that sentiment in the national board was opposed to making any change.

What do you do in a situation of this kind when an organization of which you are a member continues a racist policy? Had I known it before I joined, I would have bypassed the privilege; in fact, I would have protested St. Olaf applying for a chapter membership. Did being a member make a difference in the action that should now be taken? I decided that it did. It would be easier to exercise influence for change from the inside than from the outside. I therefore wrote the national office that as a protest against Pi Kappa Delta's racist policy, I would lay aside my key, never to wear it again until the policy would be changed. In a few years, Pi Kappa Delta dropped its racial discrimination. By that time it had become habit not to wear the key, and so it has continued to rest in a box with collar buttons and cuff links.

This racist issue in connection with honorary societies obtruded again not long after I had graduated from college. St. Olaf had been granted a chapter in Blue Key, an honorary society for students who had been adjudged as exercising leadership in the student body. A letter from Dr. E. Clifford Nelson, then active as a student to secure a Blue Key chapter at St. Olaf, announced that the organization's rules permitted a few spaces for recent alumni. He then revealed that the student committee had voted to award membership to me if I would accept it.

I was moved by the generosity of the students, and I expressed a warm thanks to Clifford Nelson. I then mentioned the experience with Pi Kappa Delta. Could he assure me that Blue Key did not draw a color line? He confessed that he did not know, but he would find out. To his great chagrin he learned that Blue Key was also racist. That left me no other resource than to thank the students again for the generous intent that prompted the offer but to say regretfully that my convictions would not allow acceptance of the honor.

In the school year 1927-28 I served the SVM as a traveling secretary. In the field visitation during the fall of '27 each campus was given information about the SVM Quadrennial Convention that would be meeting the Christmas-New Year week in Detroit.

The preparations for the Detroit Quadrennial marked the beginning of a turning point in race relations at interdenominational-international student assemblies. The committee on arrangements had gotten an agreement with the city convention bureau that any student registered for the convention, whatever his race, would be accepted at the hotels and restaurants in the city. Some weeks before the assembly, the convention bureau notified the local committee and the SVM office in New York that they were not able to deliver on their promise. The SVM New York office advised that if this were true the Quadrennial would not meet in Detroit. The convention bureau conferred again with the hotel and restaurant representatives. That resulted in a return to their first agreement.

More than 3300 delegates came from some 600 colleges and universities in Canada and the United States. A number of black students were registered. During the week no incidents occurred to make the Detroit Convention Bureau regret their agreement with the SVM. It was rumored that after the Quadrennial was over, Detroit slipped back into its old pattern of discrimination. But people had caught the glimmer of a new day on the horizon. A witness had been made.

After the Quadrennial, there was a new confrontation with the hurt of racism. I was visiting a normal school at Florence, Alabama. The students and faculty were all black. I was received courteously but with cool cordiality. At the noon hour I was invited to lunch in the principal's home. The luncheon was beautifully prepared, and the menu was an excellent illustration of a balanced and tasty meal. This was the first time I had been in the home of a black family. From every point of view I would have to give it a grade of A.

After the meal the principal invited me to return with him to his office on the campus. The conversation moved from casual talk to the race issue. I responded out of my own convictions. Suddenly, the principal turned in his swivel chair, looked me in the eyes, and asked, "Now where do you stand on this issue?"

I was taken aback by this unexpected confrontation and replied, "I thought you would have understood my position from what I have said as we have talked."

His reaction was, "Yes, but people do a lot of talking."

I realized then that words would not be sufficient to convince him. He had mentioned earlier that he might be going to summer school at the University of Minnesota. I seized upon that possibility and said, "Next summer I expect to be married. If you come to Minneapolis to study, and if you keep me informed of your arrival time, you will be as welcome in our home as any of my white friends." He thanked me and seemed satisfied that my words were backed by fraternal convictions.

In 1947 while I was serving Trinity in Brooklyn, Branch Rickey, majority owner of the Brooklyn Dodgers, announced that Jackie Robinson, a black player, had been signed to play first base. That season's first appearance of the St. Louis Cardinals, occasioned a *Brooklyn Eagle* story that the Cardinals had threatened not to take the field if Jackie should play. In reading this story I decided it was a "pastoral duty" to be present at that game. I got a seat right behind first base.

The reported threat of the Cardinals not taking the field if Jackie played was not carried out. But after the game had progressed for a couple of innings, it was clear that one of the Cardinals tried deliberately to spike Jackie. Evidently he had been coached to be alert; he withdrew his foot in time to avoid the spike, and then looked up at the Cardinal player with a big friendly smile. The entire grandstand on the first base side of the infield saw that smile and burst out with a very loud hand clap. After that no Cardinal player dared do other than accept Jackie. And, of course, his quality of play compelled respect.

Jackie Robinson's signing of a Dodger contract was a special event. For the first time the color line had been broken in major league baseball. And since then, professional sports have probably contributed more than any other single force to evaluate people on the basis of their competence rather than the color of skin. In a letter of appreciation which I wrote to Branch Rickey for his landmark contribution to defeat racism in baseball, he disavowed accepting any compliment. He said he signed Jackie Robinson purely on the basis of his skill as a ball player. But I find it interesting to remember that Branch Rickey had the reputation for being an active Christian layman in the Methodist church. And a national leader in the Methodist church who was close to Branch Rickey shared with a friend of mine the information that he was certain that Rickey's Christian convictions had played a large part in his effort to find a black player whose competence would guarantee acceptance.

When we moved to Minneapolis in 1954 I was much disappointed to find that there were no fair housing opportunities for black people. And it bothered me very much that this could be true in Minneapolis, a city of churches—a place where Lutherans were in the majority. Was this due to thoughtlessness? Or, did not Lutherans understand the Bible, the very book that was God's word for them? I decided that something had to be done about this open sore.

I contacted Dave Witheridge, the general secretary of the Greater Minneapolis Council of Churches. In him I found a kindred spirit. He agreed that removal of this blight was a task for all the churches in the city. And then he did what so often happens. If you speak up about a problem, you get drafted to take some initiative. He asked me to work with the council's Fair Housing Committee. I could not do other than answer yes.

In meeting with the committee I proposed that we have a series of open forums in different congregations in the city. This would be the beginning of an educational process. I introduced the subject in a series of the forums. Generally, the response was positive. However, one woman who attended several of the forums was always ready to speak when it was time for discussion and questions. Her contribution was the same each time: "This concern for open housing is Communism."

The forums were to be followed by an appeal to the churches to use Annual Race Relations Sunday to declare themselves; and to pray that God would move the Minneapolis citizenry to support open housing.

Dr. Witheridge and his staff took responsibility to organize the participation of all the churches. This was given public exposure in an advertisement in the *Minneapolis Tribune* on Friday, February 9, 1962, and again a year later, Friday, February 8, 1963. Practically all Christian churches and some other religious groups allowed their names to be used. In the advertisement they declared: "All doors—Open to All." And the 1963 advertisement included this strong appeal:

> This Sunday, February 10, marks the forty-first annual observance of Race Relations Sunday. The congregations listed here, and others who have preferred to express their convictions in other ways, continue their concern for a just society in which all people will have equal opportunity to develop their potentialities. We reaffirm our belief, stated by many state and national church bodies, that residential segregation makes difficult the integration of neighborhoods, churches, and other institutions. We urge citizens to cooperate with community organizations which have pledged to support nonsegregated practices in selling, buying and leasing property . . . and to follow nondiscriminatory practices in housing.

Not long after the 1963 advertisement, Sally Luther, a member of the state legislature, wrote me a letter. She reported that several efforts to get the legislature to enact a Fair Housing Law were defeated. And then she concluded that when the legislature saw where the churches stood, it was easy to get action.

One day I received a letter from a member of an ALC congregation in Wisconsin expressing surprise that I held a membership in the Minneapolis Athletic Club. His "surprise" was occasioned by his understanding that Jews were not allowed to belong. I immediately replied that he was misinformed. I could assure him that I knew several Jews who were members.

This letter caused me to look up the constitutional provision governing membership. To my horror I read that membership was open to people of the Caucasian race. This was a soft way of saying that "black people need not apply." I was surprised because I had recently had Carl Rowan, the black journalist, as a luncheon guest. Before inviting him I telephoned the club to be sure that no complications would obtrude. The answer was that there would be no problem at all.

The fact that the constitution barred other than white people as members, required an amendment; otherwise I would have to resign my membership. I went to the president of the club and explained how I felt about it. He agreed that an amendment should be introduced at the annual meeting, but suggested that I say nothing about it. If I were to contact a number of members to be sure to attend the annual meeting to support a change, it could provoke some emotionally charged opposition that might make a battle of it.

I agreed in the wisdom of his proposal. He asked his board of directors to recommend the necessary amendment for the annual meeting's consideration. This was done and the annual meeting accepted it without any protest.

Many nations have in the past regarded the United States as another South Africa in its racist feelings. During a field visit on behalf of the Lutheran World Federation, I found myself in Hungary. Whenever there is such a visit to be made in any of the churches in Eastern Europe, it is expected that you pay a call on the Minister of Religious Affairs. This I did, accompanied by our Lutheran bishop, the Rt. Rev. Zoltan Kaldy. The minister opened the conversation with a courteous welcome and then said, "We do not have as many cars in our country as you do in the United States. But our interest is in the people who ride in the cars and less so in machine transportation."

I replied, "I am happy to hear this. You have described the position of the church. Our primary concern is for people and not things." As the conversation proceeded, he made a cautious inquiry about racism in the United States. There was only one way to answer this question; namely, with openness and honesty. And so I said, "We have much sin to confess before God in the way we have dealt with the black people. But I believe we have turned a corner."

I then told him about some of the great changes that have occurred. As I cited these, I said, "We can honestly say that we are on our way into a new day." I called attention to a full-page story in the *Minneapolis Sunday Tribune* a few days before I left home. It reported on the large number of white families in Minneapolis who had adopted orphaned black children. Pictures and names of the people concerned were shown in the newspaper story. (There are, of course, many black people today who object to such adoptions; nevertheless, it does point to a change in attitude for this to be done and for the acceptance by the public.)

Mrs. Schiotz was along on this trip. When I mentioned the news story, she immediately opened her purse and took out the picture of Rebekah, a black girl that had been adopted by our daughter and son-in-law. The minister examined the picture and then took from his purse a picture of his grandchildren for us to scrutinize. There was then an exchange of words such as doting grandparents might express. As he did so, he turned to Bishop Kaldy and said, "Who in the Party would adopt a Gypsy girl?"

The next morning when Bishop Kaldy saw us off at the airport, he brought with him a gift from the Minister of Religion. The box was beautifully wrapped. As we examined it I could sense that the bishop was curious to know what the box might contain. I therefore opened the package before we boarded the plane and found a beautiful oriental cloisonne vase. When Bishop Kaldy saw it, he exclaimed, "Only a government official could buy an imported article of this kind."

When we got settled in the plane, I said to my wife, "When we leave this world, Rebekah must get this vase. I am sure that it was her story and picture that moved the Minister of Religion to give us this going-away gift."

The story of racism is not confined to South Africa and the United States. It has expressed itself in the colonial authority projected by Western nations over large parts of Africa and Asia, and over many of the island groupings in the Atlantic, Pacific, and Indian Oceans. The root of this outreach from the West to assert authority lay in the presupposition that help was needed. The indigenous people, it was reasoned, could not cope with the problem of increasing their income by making the great natural resources in their lands available to the world. They needed help. But there were also enlightened political leaders who saw that the colonial system was less a desire to help the people and more a concern for profit.

It was this insight that contributed heavily to President Woodrow Wilson's concern for the establishment of a League of Nations. His own nation did not give him full support, but many other nations did. And so in 1919 the League of Nations covenant was approved at the Versailles Peace Conference. One of the objectives of the League of Nations was to loosen the bonds of the colonial system by a mandate arrangement. Colonies were assigned to different nations under a mandate contract. The nation holding a mandate responsibility was expected to provide education and supervised practice in administration. Thus a colony could be brought forward to a day when full independence might be granted and self-government would become a fact.

The Mid-East is a good illustration of the mandate stewardship in operation. Britain held mandate powers over Iran, Iraq, Saudi Arabia, Palestine, and Transjordan. France was given mandate power over Syria and Lebanon. Both Britain and France exercised responsible supervision and brought their political wards to a relatively early day of independence. In many other parts of the world there have been notable successes. The one large exception is Namibia (Southwest Africa). South Africa has held the mandate power for over 60 years; but she has not been responsive to the desires of the people for independence.

As I write, a letter has come in from a young professor at Paulinum Theological Seminary in Karibib, Namibia. He was in one of my classes during a guest professorship in one of our colleges a couple of years ago. We became good friends at the time. In his letter he reports that for the first time their seminary has an all-African faculty. He adds, "It is my opinion that we have to stand alone to move with the spirit, the soil and soul, and the wind of change that is blowing throughout and across the African continent. . . .

"Here in Namibia the talking, the acting, singing, and beating drums are telling people that the Tarzan throne has gone down. Human made bars could not hold or the force of Babylon could not control the national aspiration toward freedom. Sometimes on daily and nightly basis we are facing hard realities of oppression but we have hope. . . . All our sisters and brothers in this country and other countries are behind our cause. Thanks for your involvement and contribution in this regard."

One can sense in this letter that the days of South Africa's refusal to exercise an accountable stewardship are over. It is only a matter of time.

When the Lutheran World Federation organized a Commission on World Missions it was realized that we carried a responsibility to encourage mission societies and church mission boards to construct a schedule that would "push" the indigenous churches into assumption of self-rule. The educational process for realizing this objective occurred through consultation. Instead of the Commission on World Missions conducting closed meetings, we invited missionary leaders from Europe and America, and indigenous leaders from Africa and Asia to sit with us.

Although they had no vote, the floor was open to all for freely expressing their points of view. Important issues were discussed until consensus resulted.

This spirit of expecting indigenous leaders to assume responsibilities spread like a leaven. Let me cite a couple of illustrations from Tanganyika. The General Administrative Committee proposed that a scholarship be granted to Pastor Stefano Moshi. It was to be for a year of study and observation in the United States. Some of the missionaries were opposed to granting a scholarship. This opposition was based in their fear that Pastor Moshi would be "spoiled" by exposure to American life. Because of division in the committee, I was asked to make the decision.

It would be foolish for an outsider to make a decision for those who were responsible to make the choice. In reply I began by recognizing that both sides were in agreement that Pastor Moshi was a good selection in terms of character, competence, and acceptance among his own people. I then asked a series of questions designed to focus attention on the responsibility for calling forth indigenous leaders in the African church. It was not long before agreement was reached and Stefano Moshi was voted a scholarship for one year of study in the United States.

To Moshi's formal study there was provided opportunity to make field trips to observe the life of the church in congregational settings. One day he asked if arrangements could be made to visit in the southern states. I wondered if his desire was fostered by eagerness to collect illustrations of racial discrimination. But whatever the reason for his request, I felt that it had to be granted. He must be allowed to see not only the church as it is, but also the life of the nation. And so arrangements were made for a visit in the southern states.

Moshi's year was soon concluded. He had made many friends for missionary work in East Africa. And he made an excellent interpreter of the United States and its churches when he got back to his own people. His return flight landed in Nairobi in

Kenya. News reporters were on hand to ply him with questions. They quested for something a bit more dramatic than what he gave them. Finally, one reporter asked a question directed toward getting some condemnation of America because of its racism. To this Moshi replied, "I did not go to the United States to study her sin; we have plenty of that here at home. I went to observe the work of the church and how it ministers to its people"—wisdom worthy of a Solomon.

In the Lutheran Missionary Council of Tanganyika (actually at that time called the General Administrative Committee for the Former German Missions) there was at least one missionary representative from each of the six areas where Lutherans were at work. There had been much discussion in the council about hastening the maturation of African leadership in the congregations. Some questioned whether Africans could be entrusted with the treasureship in a congregation. The reasoning expressed fear that African poverty and lack of experience in handling funds would constitute a severe temptation to "borrow" money from the treasury. The Rev. Martin Nordfelt, a Swedish missionary who served as the superintendent for the district known as the Southern Highlands, conducted a novel experiment.

Pastor Nordfelt reasoned that certainly the Lord wanted Africans to assume leadership responsibilities in their own congregations, even to the point of handling their own congregational funds. But they might have to be helped to assume such responsibilities. And so he set up a visitation in the various areas of the Southern Highlands. Congregational leaders, not omitting the treasurers, were summoned to meet him for a study week. He suggested that the treasurers should be accompanied by 12 assistants.

In each place where a study week was held, Missionary Nordfelt began the day with a Bible study period. Then he provided the treasurers and their assistants with instruction in elementary bookkeeping. Each assistant treasurer was also asked to keep books. From time to time when the books were to be inspected, the treasurer's accounts were compared with those of the assistant treasurers. It was as though the congregation had placed 12 crutches under the arms of their treasurer. Missionary Nordfelt told me that the experiment yielded positive results. The day had arrived for the congregations to be responsible caretakers in their own households.

From the time that the LWF Commission on World Missions held its first meeting in 1949 the work of the mission fields and churches in Africa had received considerable attention in its annual meetings. The post World War II winds were blowing all across the continent of Africa. It seemed desirable that opportunity be provided to bring representatives of African churches together for consultation and mutual self-understanding. And so CWM sponsored such a conference on the campus of the Teachers' Training School at Marangu, Tanganyika, in 1955. The living together in dormitory buildings was an education in itself. The delegates from South Africa were astounded at the freedom with which black and white people, lay and ordained, could live as one community.

His Excellency, Mr. Emmanuel Abraham, a Christian layman in the government's service in Ethiopia, stirred all the delegates with a keynote address: "What Do We Expect?" In the course of his address he encouraged his fellow Africans with the call: "Lift up your eyes and behold that your redemption is at hand." He applied this to the personal salvation in Christ for everyone who believes. And then he proceeded to relate it to national life and the hunger for independence.

While Mr. Abraham was speaking, the governor of Tanganyika (it was still a mandate colony under Britain at that time), who was in a chair on the platform, leaned over and whispered to me, "It will be a long time in coming." But there was more reality in the buoyant Christian response of the African delegates to Mr. Abraham's confident hope than in the governor's skepticism. In 1964 Tanganyika became Tanzania, an independent nation under the leadership of President Julius Nyerere.

Five years later, at the second All Africa Conference in Antsirabe, Madagascar, Dr. Arne Sovik, then director of the LWF Department of World Mission, in a backward look at Marangu, took occasion to say, ". . . The conference had no legislative authority nor official responsibility. But the Lutheran churches of Africa have not been the same since that conference, for it had the authority of its own impact upon those who attended, and through them, on others. It came as a pioneer venture in significant times."

Racism is pervasive, but is on its way out all over the world.

6

THE CHURCH PRESIDENCY

During the late winter and early spring of 1954 Lutheran pastors and lay leaders in the United States were talking a great deal about who would succeed President Aasgaard in the Evangelical Lutheran Church. The biennial convention was scheduled to meet in June of that year. The important item on the convention agenda was the election of a successor to Dr. Aasgaard. I have always had a strong feeling about elections to an office in the church. No person should by open or devious ways seek an office. This is to secularize the election process.

Not many days after I returned to New York from a CYCOM road trip, Dr. Paul Empie, the executive director of the council, called me into his office. Such visits with Dr. Empie were always friendly and informal: the director and staff worked together as friends. Empie turned to me and asked, "Do you know that your name is being seriously discussed as a likely candidate to succeed Dr. Aasgaard?

I took my appointment calendar out of my pocket. It disclosed that the ELC would be meeting in Minneapolis at the same time that the Lutheran Free Church would be in session at Thief River Falls, Minnesota. I was scheduled to be at the Free Church convention to report on Lutheran World Action and the Council's Orphaned Missions work. I reminded Dr. Empie of what he knew very well—that my call was to serve all member churches of the NLC. I could not therefore ask to be excused from the LFC convention commitment when there was no official obligation to be in Minneapolis. I concluded by saying to Empie with a smile, "If my name is placed in nomination at the ELC convention, I could not think of a better time to be absent."

About two o'clock the next morning the telephone rang in my hotel room at Thief River Falls. At the other end of the line Hjalmar Hove, the secretary of the ELC, was speaking. He announced that I had been elected president on the second ballot. Then he asked me to report to the convention as soon as possible. I replied that I would be on my way to Minneapolis as soon as my commitment to the Lutheran Free Church had been carried out.

That morning, as I spent some time in my morning prayers, it was with fear and trembling knowing what a changed future lay before me. But God lifted my spirit through the assigned Bible reading for the day, Isaiah 41:10. What better message could I have received: "Do not be afraid. I am with you. I am your God. Let nothing terrify you. I will make you strong and help you. I will protect you and save you."

When I had arrived at the convention I was surrounded by a number of friends who assured me of their intercessory support. But that which meant most to me was the good will expressed by other men who had been nominees. The friendly congratulations offered by Dr. Eastvold and Dr. Stavig provided solid encouragement. I could not then do other than believe that God's call lay in the convention's action.

Dr. Aasgaard, my predecessor, had demonstrated attitudes and conduct that were full of encouragement for me. Twenty-nine years of his life were invested as the leader of the ELC. At his last convention the church adopted a 10-paragraph resolution thanking him for what he had given to the church in his service.

Two of those paragraphs express an attitude that for me deserved emulation. I repeat them here:

> Dr. Aasgaard combines great administrative ability with a strong, deep, warm, and virile piety. Though busy with multitudinous affairs of his office, he never lost sight of the spiritual mission of the church. Though in the nature of the case, his work largely was with boards, executives, and an endless number of committees, he never forgot the basic importance of the local congregation, even the smallest and the humblest.
>
> The humble felt as much at home with him as the highest. He never lost the common touch. Often he has sat with individuals in their sorrows and their troubles. Of him it can truly be said, he has been a friend to many. He has endeavored to be fair and generous to all.

In submitting my first reports to the church, I visited as many district conventions as my schedule would accommodate. These convention sessions gave me an opportunity to meet a number of pastors and lay people.

Invitations for Sunday preaching in congregations were accepted as frequently as possible—whether it was for a special occasion or not. Much could be learned in these visits regarding the spiritual life in the congregations and the thinking of the people.

Barring something very unusual, I always attended the meeting of the district presidents. The health of congregational life and the spirit among our pastors lay open for observation in these meetings. If there were difficult problems that threatened disunity we could help one another through our discussions. During the first years of the ALC a few strident voices made accusations of unfaithfulness in seminary teaching regarding the Bible. It was then that the Holy Spirit led our church to a new sense of unity through the consultations that were initiated in the discussions of the district presidents.

The question of membership in the World Council of Churches had bothered the ELC long before I became president. The first decision of the church in 1948 was a definite no. Then in connection with the union negotiations it came before the church again in 1956, two years after I was elected. It will be recalled that the World Council of Churches (WCC) was organized at Amsterdam in Holland in 1948. All trinitarian churches had been invited to come to this first assembly and thus to be numbered among the charter members.

Most of the Lutheran churches in Europe joined the Council. In the United States the Augustana Lutheran Church, the former ALC, and the American Evangelical Lutheran Church, the United Evangelical Lutheran Church, and the United Lutheran Church in America became members. But the ELC and the Lutheran Free Church (LFC) did not accept the invitation.

When the Church Council met in 1948, it prepared a resolution similar to the one placed before the ELC convention in 1946. They asked the church to apply for membership. After a protracted debate the convention defeated the WCC resolution by a vote of 872 to 546.

The WCC issue did not get back on the ELC convention agenda until eight years later in connection with a consideration of union documents. It may be well, therefore, to interrupt our discussion of membership in the WCC to take note of what was emerging in discussions on Lutheran union.

The American Lutheran Conference came into being in 1930. The ALC, the ELC, Augustana, the LFC, and the UELC became members. They cooperated in a number of areas not covered by the National Lutheran Council. By January 1950 a proposal for union of the NLC member churches was under consideration in a meeting in Chicago where the ULCA was also represented. Later in that month the ELC Church Council gave consideration to which of several union options should be recommended for the approval of the June convention. The Council turned away from the proposal for union of NLC member churches and approved a strong recommendation for a union of the five American Lutheran Conference Churches. The ELC June convention adopted the proposal to work for a Conference union. Therewith it authorized the organization of a joint union committee to prepare the necessary union documents.

As the Joint Union Committee moved forward in preparation of the union documents, the ALC and the UELC members insisted on including in the Articles of Union a requirement that the new church apply for membership in the WCC at its constituting convention. This requirement occasioned a lot of grumbling in the ELC convention of June 1956. In an effort to clarify the background out of which the ALC and UELC delegates spoke, I read from positive statements by President Schuh and President Jersild telling what their membership in the WCC meant to them.

The comments from Presidents Schuh and Jersild were received with appreciation. But the opposition to the new church becoming a member in the WCC continued. Many were anxious to find a way whereby a decision on the issue could be deferred. In the confusion that threatened, Lay Delegate Albert Quie called for the floor. He proposed that we save the new church the trial of beginning its work with the burden of an unresolved emotional issue that could spawn new troubles in the future. He therefore moved that the ELC dispose of the problem by voting to join the WCC before the new church came into being. This suggestion commended itself to many delegates. A motion that the ELC consider joining the WCC at once was made and seconded. It was time for the lunch recess and so discussion of the motion was deferred until the afternoon.

I reminded the convention that the agenda would not permit time for more than nine short statements for each side. At the opening of the afternoon session I was given nine names for each side. Among these there were three lay delegate speakers for membership and six pastors. Those opposed numbered one lay delegate and eight pastors. I announced that I would call on the speakers for and against alternately. Before we proceeded to the discussion, the convention asked that we request Dr. T. F. Gullixson, president of Luther Theological Seminary, to lead in a prayer for God's direction in our thinking.

When the discussion concluded, delegates were asked to use their ballots for voting. The total number of ballots cast were 2119—1434 affirmative votes and 685 against. This was 21 more votes than the two-thirds required for passing. Thus the new church was assured that it could begin its life with a common mind on this important matter.

Representatives of ULCA and Augustana met in Chicago, March 28, 1955, and decided to appeal to all sister Lutheran churches to reconsider their present union plans in favor of the larger union. Their appeal received no positive answer from the three conference churches. This, then, led to plans for a union of Augustana, the American Evangelical Lutheran Church (Danish), the Finnish Evangelical Lutheran Church (Suomi Synod), and the ULCA (German). In 1962 this became the Lutheran Church in America.

The conference churches held their constituting convention in Minneapolis in April 1960. I was elected president. After this announcement, Dr. Henry Schuh, president of the former ALC, leaned over and whispered, "You have gotten hold of a lion by the tail." Dr. Schuh's fears were amiss. The Lord disposed the new church to work together with a minimum of strife and a large measure of concord and peace.

One of my cherished recollections from the constituting convention was our effort to get Dr. T. O. Burntvedt, president of the LFC to sit on the platform with us during the ceremonial actions that witnessed the birth of the new ALC. He had been along in the Joint Union Committee from the beginning. His church had just recently withdrawn against his will. It therefore seemed only appropriate that he should sit with us at the consummation of the union. For this invitation he expressed his warm thanks and then declined it, saying, "I don't like to be seen weeping in public."

If it was important to be alert about acting with humility and in love in my relations with congregations and pastors when I was elected president of the ELC, it was doubly so now. And it was important to be a friend of sister Lutheran churches, particularly the LCA that was about to be organized (1962). I resolved that in all contacts with other Lutheran churches I would be on guard to be open, truthful, and to act with courtesy and love. For all Lutheran churches there would have to be alertness to where God might be leading us in future inter-Lutheran relations.

The mid-'60s brought about a great deal of social turmoil and happenings like the Watts riots. In Chapter 5 I called attention to how the ALC dealt with the open housing issue in the Minneapolis area. But prejudice toward black people was nationwide. Therefore the Board of American Missions called together an educational conference on inner-city problems. It met June 21-23, 1967, at Augsburg College in Minneapolis. The tone of the weekend was set by the chairman of the conference, the Rev. Iver Sonnack, when he said, "This conference has been called because of the widespread conviction that the proclamation of the gospel may be overwhelmed by crises in the cities. The ALC can minister more effectively through our consultation here. Our efforts can be enlarged by such consultation."

Almost as soon as Pastor Sonnack had given expression to his topical thought, the conference erupted in some name calling. There followed a series of miscellaneous resolutions. Some of these criticized the boards of the church, saying that they were not paying any attention to the people in the inner cities.

Out of this babble of talk and resolutions a proposal emerged that recommended to the Board of American Missions that it form a 20-member committee on inner-city ministries. This was the equivalent of saying that the Board of American Missions did not have sufficient contact points with the hurts of the people. To the board's honor—instead of taking umbrage at the criticism of their work—they promised to give serious consideration to the proposal. And they did. They appointed a committee of 20 with broad representation from different parts of the church. They asked Mr. George Parks, a black businessman from Los Angeles, to serve as temporary chairman. He was a man who could feel the hurts of the black people through his own experience, but who had more perspective on life than many of those who were suffering.

The committee conducted the equivalent of an open hearing at the Augsburg College conference. This produced a consensus of what the board should transmit to the Omaha convention. At the convention the board's report received sympathetic consideration. This prompted the committee to constitute itself as a Committee on Inner-City Ministries (CICM). It became the source of many fruitful suggestions for the Board of American Missions.

There was another effort whereby the entire ALC addressed itself to the crisis issues of the day. I was asked to meet with a group of concerned people in Detroit. That meeting made me aware of a significant crisis ministry in the Roman Catholic church. In order to make his people more sensitive to inner-city needs of race and poverty, Archbishop Dearden had organized an educational effort which he called Project Hope. This seemed to suggest to me the question: "Why not a comparable effort in the ALC?" We contacted Archbishop Dearden's office to inquire whether they would object if we were to borrow their term "Project Hope." They replied that they would be complimented if we were to use it for a similar effort in the ALC.

I called a special meeting of our Church Council in February of that year. I told them that in a joint staff meeting every major board agreed that the whole church should be made aware of our Christian responsibility in facing the social issues of the day. The council authorized a concentrated effort for the ensuing summer. It was to bear the name "Project Summer Hope."

In order to absorb the questions of people from whom Project Summer Hope would seem like a reordering of the church's mission, we pointed our people to a study of prejudice made in several parts of the nation. It revealed that there was more prejudice among the people who are in church on Sunday mornings than among nonchurch members who sit at home reading the Sunday newspaper. In other words, just because people are members of a Christian church does not mean that they understand complicated social issues that have asserted themselves in the life of the nation.

On the other hand, a more careful study of people in the churches indicates that committed participants in the church membership are discerning people. They have learned to recognize that the prejudice shown toward other races and minorities is contrary to the gospel. It brings sorrow to the heart of our Lord.

Project Summer Hope was well received in the ALC. Before the summer was over the church had also been alerted to the crisis in rural churches. The movement of population was taking great numbers of people from the rural areas to the great industrial centers of the nation. A great shepherding need had been identified.

The ALC Commission on Public Communication undertook to produce a film seeking to portray and interpret Project Summer Hope. The producer, Ray Christianson of Minneapolis, entered it in an exhibition of the Public Relations Society of America. It was voted the Society's Silver Anvil Award. I am informed that to this date the ALC is the only denomination to have won the award.

About this time there was a delegation of inner-city black people who called and wanted to talk. They read something of a riot act to me. Their statement charged that we were providing no leadership for the church in understanding the crisis situation. In an instance of this kind you accept it with patience. You try to love them in Christ rather than being offended by their blindness to what the church was trying to do.

At San Antonio in 1970 I met one of these people again. He came to me in the sacristy where I was vesting for the service where I was to install my successor, Dr. Kent Knutson. This man was now a delegate to the convention. He looked me in the eyes and spoke with warmth, "I have never realized how many, many activities the church is involved in. It's been wonderful to be here and to see the church at work."

Some months after this a second person from the protest group came to me at a dinner where we were both present and said, "I want to apologize to you for some of the things I've said in the past. We are grateful for what the church has done and for the stand you have taken." This was another illustration that if we persevere patiently, speaking the truth in love, the Holy Spirit will provide many people with understanding.

The new church was on its toes to assert itself as a united church. Some thought that not enough responsibilities had been assigned to the districts. The matter was discussed in the Church Council and then referred to a special committee for evaluation with report back to the council. Through this committee's report the Church Council recommended some reorganization in the church's structure. This was submitted to the 1968 Omaha convention. The convention studied the recommendations carefully and proposed a number of revisions. These were returned to the Church Council and their committee for further study and the preparation of a finished report to the San Antonian convention in 1970.

The finished report was approved. One of the major changes called for a reduction of the number of church boards to four supervising boards. Instead of nine members on each of the boards there were to be 18, one from each of the districts. These were to be elected by the district conventions rather than by the general convention. These four principal boards were free to subdivide into smaller boards, in effect, subcommittees for handling special assignments from the parent board.

At San Antonio I had reached my retirement age. The implementation of the reorganization was therefore a responsibility for my successor, President Kent Knutson. It is my impression that the changes were well received in the church. They have more effectively channeled the will of the congregations to the ALC and its servant mission staffs.

The ferment for an all Lutheran union continues as the year 1980 begins. God has used the events we have been through since World War II to ready us for one Lutheran Church in the United States.

The National Lutheran Council was organized to serve the family of Lutheran churches that existed after World War I. But now things had changed. Both ALC and LCA were very much aware that some reorganization of the council would have to take place. And therefore—already in 1958—before ALC and LCA had been organized—Dr. Paul Empie, executive director of the NLC, proposed in his report a plan for facing the future. He suggested that NLC member bodies be convened in an open conference in the summer of 1959. The conference was also to be open to non-NLC member churches. Empie's proposal was well received and the conference he suggested was authorized.

The conference in the summer of 1959 resulted in three ensuing discussion meetings which became known as Inter-Lutheran Consultations. Missouri and the Slovak Synod participated in these meetings. A constitution was drafted for a successor agency to the NLC. By June 1966 the constitution had been approved and in November 1966 the new Lutheran Council in the USA had become a reality. This council continues as a cooperative agency and serves 95% of US Lutherans.

During this period that brought about the very welcome enlargement of Lutheran cooperation there were other concerns that increased tensions in the ALC. They were positive tensions but troublesome, nevertheless. They issued from the differing proposals favoring official declaration of pulpit and altar fellowship with LCA and LCMS. Some of these proposals were accompanied by volatile language. Often there was pressure exerted for a given advocate's point of view.

In the 1968 convention of the ALC official fellowship was declared with LCA and LCMS. Fellowship had been practiced with LCA for a number of years; the 1968 vote became an official stamp of approval.

In the case of LCMS preliminary discussions had to take place. During these discussions the participants in the two committees learned to respect and to love one another. For example, before we fashioned an agenda for our conversations, I felt it necessary to advise our Missouri brethren that we were not going to pick up every issue that had been on the agendas of our predecessors. To this comment one of their vice-presidents replied with a smile, "No, if that were to be done we would all have to apologize to one another."

The fellowship declaration vote was transmitted to Missouri during my visit to their convention at Denver in July 1969. I arrived at the Denver convention Saturday evening July 12. At the airport I learned that Dr. J. A. O. Preus had been elected president by a margin of 12 votes to succeed Dr. Oliver Harms. During the next two days I heard reports and saw material that gave evidence of a big city-like, ward political machine at work. What a jolt that was! For me such highly unevangelical action revealed that whoever was responsible for it was blind to the meaning of the gospel. This was the natural Adam gone wild. Dr. Preus has disavowed any responsibility for what happened. Often candidates are ill served by those who support them.

Monday morning while visiting with Dr. O. P. Kretzmann, president emeritus of Valparaiso University, I told him about the fellowship voted by our convention. I also shared with him my plan to announce in my greeting to their convention that afternoon. He suggested that there was little likelihood that Missouri would reciprocate and therefore advised that the whole matter be deferred for another convention. I replied, "O. P., we have waited long enough." He smiled and wished me well.

In the afternoon I brought my greeting to the convention. I made it clear that we would expect their convention to approve their committee's recommendation that fellowship be declared. I concluded my statement with an ALC greeting to their newly elected president. Then I added that we would pray that a large measure of the Spirit which possessed his predecessor would likewise dwell in his life and work. I used a number of words characterizing the spirit of Dr. Harms, such as, a love of truth and righteousness, and faithfulness to the word of God and the confessions. When I concluded, there was a standing ovation of longer duration than any I have ever received elsewhere. I could only account for it by the indirect tribute to Dr. Harms. Since the election a few days earlier they had come to know that some of the rumors that had floated about regarding President Harms had no basis in fact.

Later in the afternoon the fellowship issue was up for discussion. Someone from the floor asked how the new president felt about the matter. Dr. Preus rose slowly from his seat on the platform and said, "I think we should have fellowship, but not yet." However, when the vote came, fellowship was approved by a margin of 84 votes (522 to 438). After I returned home from Denver, one of the first to offer warm commendation and gratification at Missouri's vote was Dr. Knutson, the man who one year later was elected to be my successor.

The ferment for an all Lutheran union continues as the year 1980 begins. God has used the events that we have been through since World War II to ready us for one Lutheran church in the United States. God bless President David Preus and his colleagues as they point the way for the ALC!

7

ON INTERPRETING SCRIPTURE

DURING MY CHILDHOOD AND YOUTH the Bible was regarded as the Word of God—with no further "ifs or ands." Lutheran Bible schools were coming into being with a strong emphasis on a sufficient acquaintance with the Bible to know its message. This movement was generally well received.

Alongside of the wholesome emphasis on "Know your Bible," college and seminary students were beginning to ask questions about the nature of the Bible's authority. If there are elements in the Bible's content that may seem to disagree with the findings of science, whose word is valid?

The use of the historical-critical method in the study of Bible manuscripts seemed for some to be responsible for an erosion of biblical authority. This struck fear in the hearts of many faithful Christians. It seemed as though it was time to rush to the defense of the Bible. This surge continues to this day under several independent groups.

While I was in student work for the American Lutheran Conference, a group of young pastors who were present at the 1944 Ashram of the Lutheran Student Association of America (a national Lutheran student summer camp) discussed the desirability of having an inter-synodical seminar for discussing Contemporary Lutheran Theology. A follow-up meeting occurred at the Lutheran Educational Conference in Atlantic City in January 1945. A committee of five was named: Edgar Carlson, Bernhard Christensen, Karl Mattson, John Schmidt, and myself. The committee was charged with the responsibility to plan a first seminar session for November 1945. Since I had an office with secretarial services, I was asked to issue an invitation to a group of interested men that were nominated by the committee. It was understood that each person would be responsible for his own expenses.

There were a few years when the seminar met twice a year; but most of the time it was annually. At the first meeting the topic for discussion was "The Word of God and Lutheran Theology." This subject continued to get attention in subsequent meetings.

The seminary group met over a period of 20 years. At the last session in 1965, E. C. Fendt, then the recording secretary, appended this paragraph evaluation: "The historians will never be able to fully measure or evaluate the work of this group during its 20-year history. Its contribution and impact on Lutheran unity in America are not recorded in its minutes. Only the annals of God can reveal what the understanding and fellowship promoted and experienced within the group has meant for American Lutheranism in the last two decades. It served its purpose and God blessed its activity."

For those who were a part of this group, the Lutheran theological position with regard to the Word became clear. Neither

Luther nor the symbolical writings of the Lutheran church had placed any emphasis on the inerrancy of the text. For Lutherans, the Bible's central message is one of salvation by grace through faith in Jesus Christ.

This central emphasis is impressively pictured by Lucas Cranach, the great painter of the Reformation period. In July 1966 I visited Wittenberg in East Germany. My guide was Professor Thulin of Wittenberg University, an expert in Luther studies. He said to me, "One may regard Lucas Cranach as one of the foremost proclaimers of the Reformation period. The truths which the Reformers expressed in speech and in the printed word were made effectively visible through the art of Lucas Cranach."

In the city church of Wittenberg, there is a large altar painting showing Luther in the pulpit, one hand on the open Bible, the index finger of the other hand pointing to Christ on the cross, and beyond Christ is the congregation. This becomes a dramatic way wherein the painter emphasizes that the Scriptures are a means. They point to Christ, even as John the Baptist said, "Behold the Lamb of God who takes away the sin of the world." How beautifully Cranach's painting gives expression to the purpose St. John declared in recording his Gospel. You will recall the last two verses in the 20th chapter: "Now Jesus did many other signs in the presence of the disciples, which are not written in this book; but these are written that you may believe that Jesus is the Christ, the Son of God, and that believing you may have life in his name."

I have a facsimile page from Luther's translation of the Scriptures given me by the Württemberg Bible Society in Stuttgart. It is in Luther's own handwriting. When you look at it, you are reminded of the first draft of a freshman's essay. Words have been crossed out and supplanted by others. In some instances there is a second correction. This page tells the story of a Luther who pondered over the original text, not hesitating to use different words if thereby the truth might be given more faithful translation. But there are Christians in Germany who swear by Luther's translation; and if it is in any way altered through the insights provided by contemporary research, it would be regarded as tampering with the Word.

The Lutheran emphasis on the teaching concerning Scripture does two very necessary things for us. First of all, it saves us from deifying the book. (The Mohammedans have deified the Koran.) And secondly, it frees us from the fear of historical criticism.

For the laity's sake, let me say that we have no complete original Bible. The Bible we have is the result of careful study of thousands of manuscripts. The American Bible Society estimates that the study has involved 5,000 Greek manuscripts, 8,000 Latin manuscripts, and 1,000 Armenian manuscripts. None of the manuscripts are complete. One manuscript may present a whole book or parts of a book in the Bible.

Since World War II archaeologists have uncovered much new material that has a bearing on the Bible text. In order that this might be properly evaluated, the American Bible Society, the British Foreign Bible Society, the Netherlands Bible Society, and the Württemberg Bible Society have collaborated in setting up an international team of 43 well-known biblical scholars. These men were at work for 12 years and through their work the Bible societies were able in May 1965 to publish a new Greek New Testament. This is now used by translators as the basic Greek New Testament.

In referring to this new edition in Greek, a layman asked Dr. Robert Markham of the American Bible Society's translations department, "What goes into the making of a new edition of the New Testament in Greek?" After a few moments of thought, Dr. Markham replied, "This edition is made up of many ancient parts. Some came from Egyptian rubbish heaps, some from a wastebasket in a Mount Sinai monastery. Some from an almost illegible Greek manuscript in Tiflis in the Soviet Union. Still other parts were from a New York City museum and the private library of a Swiss banker. And then there were countless fragments viewed on thousands of spools of microfilm."

When I consider these facts, I am moved to bow in thanksgiving to God that there are scores of men who with great patience have worked and sweated in order that we might have the dependable text that is ours today.

Let us now turn to the American Lutheran Church and its teaching regarding the Bible. The constitution states, "The American Lutheran Church accepts all the canonical books of the Old and New Testament as a whole and in all their parts as the divinely inspired, revealed, and inerrant word of God, and submits to this as the only infallible authority in all matters of life." The ALC holds that the inerrancy referred to here does not apply to the text but to the truths revealed for our faith, doctrine, and life. The ALC has not voted this statement in a general convention. I base this interpretation on a number of factors.

First of all, the four antecedent churches did not use the word "inerrancy" in their constitutional statements although the former ALC had a footnote wherein this was used. The United Testimony does not use the word "inerrancy" in the absolute sense, but calls the Bible "the only inerrant and completely adequate source and norm of Christian doctrine and life." And it must be remembered that the United Testimony was prepared several years before the constitution was written. In fact, it was the adoption of this document by the negotiating churches that led to the authorization for the organization of a joint union committee.

I was not a member of the Joint Union Committee when the constitution was written. But it fell to my lot to interpret it for those who asked questions about its meaning. Within the first week after the ALC began to function as a church, one of the very able division heads on the new staff inquired about the meaning of inerrancy as it is used in the constitution. And then he added, "If it means that the biblical *text* is inerrant, I cannot honestly carry out the responsibilities of my office." I asked if he could accept the United Testimony's position that the "inerrancy" refers to the Bible as the dependable source for Christian doctrine and life. This he could accept, and he has served the church with great competence ever since. And always he has been a dependable Lutheran witness to the Christian faith.

The United Testimony has several long paragraphs concerning the Word. Observe these meaningful sentences: "The Bible is the Word of God given by inspiration of the Holy Spirit through human personalities in the course of human history. For the prophecy came not in old time by the will of man but holy men of God spake as they were moved by the Holy Ghost. We acknowledge with humble gratitude the condescending love of God in speaking to men through the agency of human language" (here we have echoes of Chrysostom and Luther). "We reject all rationalizing processes which would explain away either the divine or the human factor in the Bible." Any position that turns away from the paradox of a divine-human book our church labels as rationalizing.

On the way of helping our people come to an understanding of the freedom and joy in the Lutheran position with regard to the Bible, it is important to recall some of the rough water we have been through along the way. In the latter part of the 1950s, some of the district presidents in the former ELC expressed doubts about the dependability of some of the professors at Luther Theological Seminary. I proposed that instead of harboring such thoughts on hearsay, why not authorize some group conversation with all the professors. This commended itself to the district presidents and I was asked to proceed with the arrangements.

I approached President Alvin Rogness of Luther Seminary. He welcomed the possibility of such conversation. Thereupon he and I arranged for a two-day retreat at the Lutheran Bible Institute's summer camp grounds at Mt. Carmel, near Alexandria, Minnesota.

Our retreat was opened with a general introductory lecture. Then the faculty and district presidents were divided into groups of six or eight with equal representation from both sides. In these small groups there was plenty of opportunity to look one another in the eyes and to speak openly in posing questions or making statements.

The last session was a plenary meeting. Each group reported on what had transpired in its conversations. I recall how vividly the sainted Dr. George Aus unloaded a confession. With his hands in his two hip pockets he walked back and forth before the assembled group. He said that he had inherited from his home congregation of Trinity Lutheran Church in Brooklyn, a firm conviction that the biblical text was inerrant. To hold anything different would have been unfaithful. But then he went for some graduate study at the Independent Theological Faculty, the conservative seminary in Norway, presided over by the respected Professor Ole Hallesby. When Dr. Aus identified his position on textual inerrancy, he was told, "You can't hold a theological position like that." Thereafter he found peace and freedom in the Lutheran position on the Scriptures.

At the conclusion of the retreat no one had to explain that a new unity had emerged. Trust and confidence in the faculty had been conferred on the district presidents. And the faculty had received a new appreciation of the shepherding responsibilities of the bishops.

The American Lutheran Church came into being in 1960 and began functioning as the united church body January 1, 1961.

We had not moved along very far before some of the same tensions between district presidents and theological faculty professors that had appeared in the ELC became manifest. I told the district presidents about the retreat that had been held in the ELC a few years before the union. I went on to explain what a gratifying experience it had been. When the district presidents heard this they asked that a similar friendly confrontation be arranged. I discussed it with the seminary presidents of Columbus, Dubuque, St. Paul, and Saskatoon. They immediately gave their approval.

This ALC retreat involved many more participants than we had in the ELC meeting. But we used the same program format. Once again God conferred rich blessings on all the participants. When we adjourned, we sensed a unity in faith and purpose that was exhilarating. The new church was united at a depth that went far beyond what the new corporate structure could define.

In the North Pacific District there were some pastors whose fears about the church's position with regard to the Bible was similar to that of some of the district presidents before the two retreats had been held. These pastors and some lay people adopted for themselves the name "Lutherans Alert." They demanded of their district president, Dr. S. C. Siefkes, that he should make room for a lecture on the Bible at the 1966 district convention. But they specified that the speaker could not be one of the theological professors.

Confronted with this demand, Dr. Siefkes telephoned to me and asked me to give the lecture. I reminded him that we were already in the district convention season and I would be on the road almost continuously. But Dr. Siefkes would not relent, adding that no one could object to my speaking because of my office. And so I had to yield.

In 1966 there was still excellent train service. I reserved a roomette on the North Coast Limited for privacy and study. My lecture was written on my way out to Tacoma. The convention was very attentive while I spoke. After a short period for questions, the delegates recessed for discussion in small groups. In the group with which I met, one layman got up and identified himself as a member of the national board of "Lutherans Alert." And then he concluded, "If what you said to the convention is the position of the ALC, I don't know why we have 'Lutherans Alert.' "

Ten days after the Tacoma convention the ALC Church Council was in session at Winnipeg. They voted to have the Tacoma address printed in full and distributed to all the pastors of the ALC. The Board of Theological Education continued for some time to make the address available on request.

Two years before the Winnipeg meeting of the Church Council, one of the districts had memorialized the Church Council to prepare a statement in response to questions that had been raised about the church's doctrinal position. The council appointed a committee consisting of the three U.S. seminary presidents and four district presidents (Drs. Daehlin, Huffman, Mohr, and Nelson). The committee reported to the Winnipeg meeting. The council adopted the report unanimously and submitted it to the ALC convention in October 1966 under the title *Statement on Doctrinal Concerns*. The statement begins by quoting from the United Testimony in the section, "The Means of Grace, the Word and the Sacraments." The statement then follows with these paragraphs:

1. The American Lutheran Church encourages intensive and honest scholarship in all areas of knowledge relating to the faith. It acknowledges as its duty under God to speak to each generation with the fullest possible consideration of the alternatives which threaten to distort or deny the faith once delivered to the saints. It is committed to avoid all rationalizing which would explain away either the divine or the human factors which the Holy Spirit has used in revealing God's will for mankind.

2. Responsible stewardship of the gospel demands that our teachers and pastors regard seriously the concepts and language which have been in traditional use in the life of the church and that they avoid the offense which may be caused by language which creates confusion and doubt over against the declared faith of the church. When new forms or language are used, care must be exercised that the great truths of the church's confession be not undermined.

3. The American Lutheran Church adheres firmly to the principle that every interpretation of Scripture must be in accord with Scripture and rejoices, therefore, in the earnest and painstaking efforts that are being pursued by its teachers and pastors to determine precisely what God is saying to his people in the Bible.

4. The American Lutheran Church declares that to determine what is distinctively Lutheran in the teachings of the church, the norm must be the confessions or symbols which for centuries have been definitive for the Lutheran family. To contend or imply that to be a Lutheran one must subscribe to something more or less than the confessions themselves is to demand something other of a teacher or a pastor than is required by the constitution of the church.

5. The American Lutheran Church believes that the Holy Spirit does not abandon the church. He inspires its search for truth and he strengthens its members in their love of one another. Within the great unity that they all have in Christ as Lord and Savior, he tolerates and even encourages a plurality of emphases which indeed adds to the riches of the church's life. It is in this confidence of the Holy Spirit that the church prays for an increase of both love of the brother and in unity in the faith.

In the light of these affirmations we add the following observations:

a) Knowing that the devil is pleased to have the church dislodged from the pure teaching of the gospel, The American Lutheran Church urges upon its pastors and teachers the utmost vigilance that God's Word be taught and proclaimed in such a way that souls are brought to conviction of sin, to repentance and to the joy of forgiveness and to the new obedience which is in Christ.

b) The American Lutheran Church deplores the confusion that is created by the disdainful use of such terms as orthodoxy, neoorthodoxy, the new theology, liberalism, rationalism, pietism, fundamentalism, modernism, and believes that the church will best be served if pastors and teachers avoid using any label in their mutual search for the message of Scripture and in speaking of one another's efforts.

c) Although redeemed and restored to fellowship with God through Jesus Christ, the believer still lives in the limitations of the Old Adam. His sanctification never achieves perfection in this life. His will cannot attain perfect holiness nor can his mind attain perfect knowledge. His best efforts to formulate a theology in terms of propositions and statements will fall short. To assure that the church can arrive at human concepts or expressions that are in every respect correct is as much a symptom of pride as to assume that the church or its members can achieve sinlessness in their daily lives. Both in living the faith and in knowing or expressing the faith, we all need daily forgiveness and amendment which the Holy Spirit alone can give.

d) The American Lutheran Church is grateful for the vigor of theological endeavor among its teachers, and also for the responding concern for theological integrity among its pastors and people. Let no one hold a brother in disdain, nor charge him with either obstinacy or unfaithfulness without first exploring in love a basis for understanding. Mutual trust is a priceless treasure and is basic to genuine fellowship in the church. If brothers who differ or seem to differ in theological expression will in charity "put the best construction" on what is said and done, the church will grow together in the life which we all share in Christ Jesus, our Lord, and sound, historical, biblical doctrine will be affirmed among us.

The Board of Parish Education and the Board of Publication had been alert to the retreat meeting of the district presidents and the three seminary faculties. They had also observed the blessings it had given to all the participants in the retreat. This awakened in the Board of Parish Education staff the possibilities for assisting our congregations to experience that the "Scripture

Still Has Power Today." Therefore they prepared and published a study discussion book of 161 pages titled, *The Bible: Book of Faith.*

Dr. C. Richard Evenson, director of the Board of Parish Education at the time the book was published, concludes his introduction with these two paragraphs:

> This book of essays is intended primarily for use in a course of study by church school teachers and adult leaders in the congregation. There has been a great increase of knowledge about the Bible in recent years. Responsible leaders should be informed by what is known at the present time. All of us who use and teach the Bible need to deepen our understanding of both the nature and message of our great heritage.
>
> It is the sincere prayer of the Board of Parish Education that this little volume, and the studies it will occasion, may aid every person using it to a deeper understanding of the Bible and to a firmer commitment to Jesus Christ, the Word of God incarnate.

8

THE LUTHERAN CHURCH AND GLOBAL RELATIONSHIPS

The Protestant Reformation moved through the Germanic and Scandinavian countries largely on the teachings of Martin Luther. In a number of instances the Lutheran churches became state supported. But for many years there was little contact with each other across national boundaries.

In the last quarter of the 19th century a sense of family began to emerge in Germany. It resulted in the organization of the German Evangelical Lutheran Conference and brought together the leaders of the churches at intervals of several years; their concern was largely for doctrinal issues.

In the Scandinavian countries contact across national boundaries began in the middle of the 19th century. There was considerable interchange among deaconess motherhouses, Lutheran bishops, clergy associations, Lutheran students, and in foreign missions. During the first quarter of the 20th century, representatives from Denmark, Norway, and Sweden met with the German Evangelical Lutheran Conference. But the awareness of the Lutheran family was limited to Europe.

We have all observed that some communities of people might live for years without any real awareness of their neighbors. But if serious illness strikes, families discover their neighbors overnight. The beginning of a world family awareness among Lutherans happened very much in the same way.

In the United States the National Lutheran Council (NLC) was organized in 1918. It became the means of focusing the attention of its member churches on the post World War I needs among European Lutherans. Funds were raised and American commissioners administered the relief and reconstruction money in 18 different countries. In doing this work these men experienced a strong feeling of fellowship with their Lutheran brethren in Europe. Some of these commissioners thought it would be well "to form a world federation of Lutheran churches for mutual encouragement and support."

Dr. John A. Morehead, who headed the team of commissioners to Europe, reported the proposal to form a world federation of Lutheran churches to the NLC in 1919. The idea commended itself to the NLC and it appointed a committee to draft plans for a world association. They were instructed to consult with European church leaders in the preparation of their plans.

Thus it came to be that the NLC and the German Evangelical Conference issued a joint invitation to all Lutheran churches to meet in Eisenach in Germany, August 19-26, 1923, for the constituting meeting of the Lutheran World Convention (LWC). The 151 delegates represented 22 countries, but thousands of visitors were present to give evidence of their strong interest. The number of delegates was kept small so that there might be ample opportunity for them to get acquainted with one another. Awareness of a global Lutheran family was taking shape.

Bishop Ludwig Ihmels of Saxony presided at the Eisenach sessions. Formal papers were presented; discussion centered on the Lutheran confessions, foreign mission problems, plans and progress on international relief, the ecumenical character of Lutheranism, and what Lutherans can contribute to Christian unity. A brief but inclusive doctrinal statement was adopted.

The organization that was set up chose the name Lutheran World Convention. It provided for two ongoing administrative committees: a large one that was charged with maintaining contact with Lutheran populations in different countries, and an executive committee of six members—two from Germany, two from the Scandinavian countries, and two from America. Dr. John A. Morehead was named chairman of the executive committee.

The executive committee met annually in different European centers. They were charged with administration of relief—particularly to Lutherans in Russia, and the preparation of plans for a second Lutheran World Convention meeting in six years. Plans were also made for a worldwide celebration of the 400th anniversary of Luther's Catechism in 1929 and the 400th anniversary of the Augsburg Confession in 1930. As I now write the worldwide Lutheran family is busy with plans for an ecumenical observance of the 450th anniversary in 1980.

The second LWC general meeting was held in Copenhagen, Denmark in 1929. There were 149 delegates from 43 churches in attendance. The election of Dr. John A. Morehead, well-known among the Europeans and the executive secretary for the NLC, to the presidency was very well received.

The third general meeting of the LWC met in Paris. There were 90 delegates from 43 churches registered. These were largely church officials and advisers. Bishop A. Marahrens of Saxony was elected president. Dr. F. H. Knubel, president of the United Lutheran Church in America, became the vice-president.

Dr. Knubel had discerned the warm family spirit that existed among the delegates at Paris. But he had also recognized that if this relationship was to endure, something more than the loosely organized LWC must be brought into being. He therefore introduced a resolution providing for a reorganization. In doing this he made the purpose very specific: "to bring Lutheran churches and organizations of the world into an enduring relationship with one another in order to promote oneness of faith and confession and to ward off antagonistic and hostile influences." The resolution was welcomed with a strong vote of approval.

After the Paris meeting, the executive committee decided to hold the next general meeting of the LWC in Philadelphia. All were pleased with the prospect of a gathering in the new world. But it didn't come to pass; in September 1939 World War II burst upon Europe.

It is important that we recall what disturbed international relations during the years after World War I. The meetings at Eisenach, Copenhagen, and Paris were convened when the world lay in a valley of many shadows. World War I was concluded by the Versailles Peace Treaty, often referred to as the "iniquitous Versailles Treaty." Under the leadership of Prime Minister Clemenceau of France and Winston Churchill of Great Britain, there was an insistence on punishing Germany for the attack initiated by Kaiser Wilhelm's armies in the summer of 1914. The heavy indemnity exacted of Germany by the Peace Treaty placed an economic yoke of such weight that it almost strangled the nation. The severe depression that followed paved the way for the rise of the Nazi Party.

Hitler and his Party could rule by decree; and he repudiated the Versailles Treaty and took other actions that released the business world from its economic paralysis. Living conditions in the life of the nation improved. People who had been without work once again had jobs. Hitler blamed the Versailles Treaty and the Jews for what Germany had suffered. Under such conditions the nation was solidified by the Nazi-inspired hatreds. But Auschwitz and its horrors were better known outside Germany than within the nation.

However, in time information about the persecution of the Jews filtered through to the German people. But the Nazi Party and its secret police kept the people in terror of speaking out. This failure became an oppressive load of guilt for many people, particularly the church leaders.

During the war years the executive committee members of the LWC had no opportunity for effective communication with one another. It became a responsibility of the American section of the LWC to gather and administer funds for orphaned missions, refugees, and European relief. And it was done gladly. But already the American leaders were looking forward to the restoration of the partnership with the leaders in the European section of the LWC. Therefore, before the war was over, early in 1945, Dr. Ralph Long and President P. O. Bersell were sent to Europe by the National Lutheran Council to prepare for the reactivation of the LWC. They found little enthusiasm for this among the Scandinavians. The war had cooled their sense of Lutheran familyhood.

A few months later in the fall of 1945 the American section of the LWC sent Dr. Long, President Fry of the ULCA, and President Aasgaard of the ELC to try once again to infuse the LWC with new life. They recognized that it could not happen under German leadership. And so they prevailed on Bishop Marahrens to resign his presidency of the LWC. They then asked Archbishop Eidem of neutral Sweden to serve as acting president.

The Lutheran World Federation Is Born

In July 1946 the executive committee of the LWC met in Sweden and changed the status of Archbishop Eidem from acting president to an elected president. The executive committee recognized that postwar feelings and economic conditions would not permit carrying out the Paris Assembly's decision to hold the next meeting in the USA. It was agreed that it should be at Lund in Sweden in the summer of 1947.

Lund was the first international church assembly to be held after the war. Some thought it was too soon. I was present as a delegate from the ELC—my first such experience. And I was on the alert to watch whether Christ or postwar antipathies would govern the convention's mood.

As the delegates filed in during the opening session, their faces reflected a solemn spirit. I studied the German delegates carefully. But their faces showed a quizzical look as if to say, "Will we be received as brethren? Or will we be catechized to establish blame for all the sins of our nation?" I was in a quandary until it came to singing "A Mighty Fortress Is Our God." Never had I heard it sung with such conviction; whatever the language, whether it was sung in Swedish, Norwegian, German or English, all voices blended into a moving confession of faith. After this session my heart was at rest. I knew that Christ was present and that his will would prevail.

As the days moved on, the Assembly seemed to absorb a spirit of freedom and positive informality. I thought this came strongly to the fore in a session where Dr. Fry was reading a committee report with a series of resolutions. One of these expressed the confidence: "We believe that God wants the lay people in the church to be active." Suddenly Herman Ochs, a delegate from San Antonio, Texas, boomed out from the back of the room, "Mr. Chairman." Without waiting to be recognized, he strode with long steps to the front until he stood beside Archbishop Eidem of Sweden, who was chairing that session. Standing beside the archbishop he proceeded to say, "We do not need to say that we *believe* God wants lay people to be active in the church," we can say, "We *know* that he wants this."

Then shaking his finger at the Archbishop, he added, "You, Mr. Archbishop," and turning to the Assembly, he said, "and you other bishops and pastors, you are not the church by yourselves. All of us together are the church." When he paused, Eidem took one step toward the very tall Herman Ochs (Eidem was a short man) and standing on tiptoes, he threw his arms around the American layman's neck, pulled his head down and kissed him on the cheek. The assembly burst out in clapping. Later, Dr. Fry was heard commenting, "Veto by embrace."

This friendly informality with alert concern for the administrative policies of the Federation was ably nurtured by Dr. S. C. Michelfelder, the executive secretary. No one could meet Dr. Michelfelder without quickly recognizing his great gifts and his marked capacity for friendship with all whom he might encounter. And these gifts of the first executive secretary reappeared with variations in his successors, Dr. Carl Lund-Quist, Dr. Kurt Schmidt-Clausen, Dr. Andre Appel, and Dr. Carl Mau. It all added up to recognition and appreciation for global family awareness that took hold of Lutherans in all parts of the world.

The Federation was blessed in its choice of the first president, Bishop Anders Nygren. In him God gave the Federation a man of well-recognized competence as a biblical theologian. His definitive work, *Agape and Eros,* became a biblical and philosophical discerning of the difference between agape and eros. Eros is the natural human affection that is caused; agape is divine love, spontaneous and "uncaused."

"Why does God love? There is only one right answer: Because it is his nature to love." This understanding of God's love seemed to get lost in the church of the Middle Ages. With the coming of the Reformation it once again came to the fore. Luther's gospel proclamation, his emphasis on justification by faith, revealed Christ as the Divine Agape. The Divine Love calls forth in the believer a love of God committed to the doing of his will.

During the years that I was in student work I found that a

number of the pastors involved in a ministry to students found great stimulus in the writings of Bishop Nygren.

The years immediately preceding Lund saw new trials for some of the churches that were in countries where Russia had asserted her control. In visiting these areas on behalf of the LWF I heard many stories of remarkable Christian witness under conditions of great testing. One of these which I consider unique and also somewhat representative is the story of Archbishop Jaan Kiivit when I visited the Estonian church.

In the fall of 1944 the German army retreated before the advancing Soviet forces. Estonian Christians were well acquainted with the difficulties that the church would face. And so, while there was yet time thousands fled to Germany and Sweden.

Pastor Kiivit was strongly tempted to flee. But it seemed to him that the decision had to be made in prayer and reflection. And this resulted in a conviction that he must stay. He told me that at the last meeting of the city's Lutheran ministerium before the Soviet army took over, he explained to his fellow pastors the choice that he had made. He told them that if he were assured that he could take his parishioners with him, he would flee at once. But this was an impossibility. And so, as a shepherd of the flock he had been called to serve, he felt compelled to stay. Then he added that they must not feel compelled to follow his choice. Each pastor would have to follow the leading God would give him.

After hearing this story and after the opportunity to visit with him, I was not surprised that the church had voted Kiivit the responsibility of bishop and then archbishop.

The physical relief needs of Lutheran churches in Europe and in Africa and Asia elicited an outpouring of gifts. This activity kept the Lutheran family alive among both the giving and receiving churches. It asserted itself increasingly in the assemblies of the LWF.

The second assembly was held in Hanover, Germany, in 1952. The warm reception by the host church of Hanover was visibly illustrated by the genial spirit of the Hanoverian bishop, the Right Reverend Hanns Lilje. Tens of thousands of visitors came from the East European countries. Under the theme "The Living Word in a Responsible Church," the assembly discussion groups and the worship periods contributed much to the fellowship of Lutherans in Hanover. The climax came in the last worship service where 65,000 Lutherans joined in a fellowship of confession and witness.

There was enough concern for lay people being well represented in the life of the LWF that the constitution was amended to increase the size of the executive committee from 16 to 20. These extra spaces were to be filled by lay people.

This assembly girded itself for a broad range of services for its member churches. Executive departments of Theology, World Mission, and World Service were authorized. The sense of world family identity asserted itself further in the provision for the publication of an LWF Encyclopedia. Professor Julius Bodensieck of Wartburg Theological Seminary at Dubuque, Iowa, was asked to assume responsibility for the editorship. Dr. Bodensieck carried out his commitment so well that in 1965 Augsburg Publishing House could place on the market three volumes under the title of *The Encyclopedia of the Lutheran Church.* These three resource books are so well organized and usable that every Lutheran congregational library should have a set.

The Third Assembly met in Minneapolis in the summer of 1957 under the theme "Christ Frees and Unites." The reports from the discussion groups at Hanover had been edited and made available in a book of 51 theses. This book became the tool for the discussion groups at Minneapolis. It provided an excellent summary of the faith that confers familyhood on Lutherans in the world.

A few days before the assembly I was contacted by a staff member in the offices of the ALC. He reported that there were many people who were disturbed about Dr. Fry being the nominee to succeed Bishop Lilje as the president of the LWF. Since Dr. Fry was already chairman of the Central Committee of the WCC, this person reasoned that it would be too much concentration of power for the same person to hold these two important ecumenical offices at the same time. Then he added that there were people who wanted me to be the next president of the LWF and that my name would be offered in nomination from the floor. As a clincher he said that the representatives from the Younger Churches would support such a nomination.

I told my informant that I could not give my approval for any such action. And then I warned that in my judgment nothing but trouble would result from what he proposed. But as the time moved on I heard things that made it clear that the promotion of my name was continuing. This disturbed me much.

I knew Dr. Fry very well. He had been chairman of CYCOM the six years I served as its executive secretary. I had a good deal of affection for him and I regarded him as one of the ablest leaders in the whole Christian church. Normally, a nominee who had been so much a part of the LWF leadership from the beginning would easily be elected. But the ALC staff member's reference to the Younger Church leaders confused me. I had many friends among them and no one can be sure what will happen when feelings are stirred.

As I thought about this with my ear cocked to heaven, I resolved that I must get the floor in the assembly the moment that Fry's name would be submitted in nomination. This I did and spoke some strong words of support. I then added that it had been called to my attention that some were opposed to Fry's nomination because he was already chairman of the Central Committee of the WCC. I said that I regarded this as a personal decision for Dr. Fry. His great gifts conferred on him a phenomenal capacity for work and getting things done. If he felt that he could handle both offices, that would be just another way for his rich gifts to be shared on a still wider front.

After I had spoken the men who were going to submit my name in nomination remained silent. Dr. Fry was elected by the Federation's very decisive vote.

During the five years between Hanover and Minneapolis the Federation's income increased fourfold. And the healing ministry totaled over $200,000,000 in cash and goods.

The German National Committee asked that the Department of Theology should be requested to study the possibility of organizing an institute for confessional research. It was presented by Bishop Dietzfelbinger of Bavaria. He reported that relationships between Roman Catholic churches and Lutherans in his diocese had improved tremendously. He felt that it was time for the LWF to be doing something about the opportunity which he felt lay before us in the current friendly attitude of the Roman Catholic Church.

One of the moving spirits in support of Bishop Dietzfelbinger's proposal was Professor Kristian Skydsgaard, a theologian on the faculty of the University of Copenhagen. Skydsgaard was well acquainted with Roman Catholic theology. He had been a speaker in a number of ecumenical seminars. And he was a man of irenic temperament, a real apostle of love. His support was determinative for many leaders in the Federation's member churches.

A year after the Minneapolis assembly the Executive Committee of the Federation authorized the Department of Theology to proceed with the organization of the institute. This was done and it was located at Strasbourg, France, a city with strong Lutheran and Catholic parishes. Professor Skydsgaard was elected chairman of the board.

The Fourth Assembly was convened in Helsinki, Finland, under the theme "Christ Today." This topic was pointed toward a focus on the Lutheran emphasis on justification. In the volume of *Helsinki Reports,* the Department of Theology sought to set forth a clear understanding of justification in today's world. The following paragraph, one among 93, is illustrative of the quality of the discussion:

> There is the self-righteousness of some orthodox Lutherans. They stand firmly in the theological heritage of the Reformation, vigorously opposing all Romanist, Reformed, or Anabaptist tendencies. They are zealous for pure doctrine and strenuous defenders of the authority of the Scriptures. But they suspect that the Lord has a special affection for them because of their devotion to His cause, their clear reasoning, effectiveness in argument, and consistent suspicion of all contemporary learning. For all their good intentions, they are in danger of confusing theology and faith and of making theological dialectics a way of salvation. (From Fourth Assembly document number 3 "On Justification," paragraph 42.)

The churches of Africa and Asia participated in the discussion periods without hesitation. They demanded that the theological focus must be on the problems of today. There were some constitutional amendments made at this assembly. It was obvious that the delegates did not want the world Lutheran family to drift into the formation of a world church. And they did not wish the Federation to assume churchly functions.

Eleven new churches were received into membership at Helsinki.

The Matins, Vespers, and Communion services were unusually well attended. This led many people to refer to Helsinki as the worshiping assembly. We were happy that this was true for we had a number of official visitors present—with the Lutheran Church–Missouri Synod and the Roman Catholic Church well represented.

Each assembly has the responsibility of electing new officers. Bishop Smemo of Norway had been asked to serve as chairman of the nominations committee. He came to me and reported that his committee had pretty well agreed that they were going to present my name for president to succeed Dr. Fry. Immediately I answered, "Bishop Smemo, since an American is the current president it would probably be best to find someone other than an American. We must not forget that the LWF is a world family of churches."

But when the nominations committee reported to the delegates, my name was submitted.

A long time after the assembly had adjourned, I learned that an official visitor had encountered a lady in the vestibule of the church where the assembly was in session. It was during the business meeting. This lady turned to the official visitor and inquired whether he knew who might be elected president. He answered, "I think it will be Dr. Schiotz of the ALC."

This reply elicited from the lady who had asked the question, "Oh dear, I hope not!" Later, the official visitor learned that this lady was Mrs. Schiotz. He then understood her lack of enthusiasm for the expressed likelihood of my election.

Lutheran Churches in Communist Countries

The Sunday after my election I was installed into office during a large festival service on a big athletic field. After the service many came up to talk. Among these were three bishops from churches in Eastern Europe. Their concern was that I should visit them sometime soon. I had noted that the visit of the LWF president in the member churches stirred an awareness of family fellowship. I shall share some facets from three of these visits.

Bishop Andrew Wantula of Poland came to me with apparent hesitance and asked, "Do you have any love for us?"

I replied, "If I didn't have love for you, I couldn't call myself a disciple of Christ." Then he smiled and invited me to visit their church in Poland.

When the day came, Bishop Wantula was very helpful in assisting me to understand the government attitude toward the churches in the countries of Eastern Europe. He said, "You must always remember that a communist state is atheistically oriented. In principle it is opposed to the Christian church and to all religions. But, while you must never forget this, you must not assume that communist countries don't allow some religious work to be carried on. In fact, in some countries they may even contribute to the salary of pastors. But you must not assume that what you find in one communist country will be the same in others. The government may even vary its handling of relationships with the church from place to place in the same country."

I found that what Bishop Wantula told me was more helpful than any other observations that were shared with me.

Whenever you enter a communist country to visit the churches you relate to the Minister of Ecclesiastical Affairs. I was booked to visit Bratislava in Czechoslovakia. The bishop had arranged for an appointment with the Minister of Ecclesiastical Affairs. When we came to his office building, he was standing outside his door with an assistant at his side.

Both men were standing as erect as though they were on military parade. We shook hands and were ushered into his office. We began our conversation with comments about the weather. But I wanted to get down to something more substantive. I was eager to get some revelation of how he felt about the Christian faith. I had noted that Bratislava was growing as a city. And so I said, "Mr. Minister, I observe that in the growth of your city some communities are far removed from the regular churches. Are you providing permits and some help for the erection of new church buildings?"

He replied, "I could answer that in a principle way or in a practical way." Then he hesitated for a moment and said, "I think I had better answer in a practical way. We have streetcars and buses; people can use them to get to the churches in the city proper."

Then, as though he recognized that the "practical" answer to my question was no answer at all, he paused and said, "Maybe I ought to answer it in a principle way." And then he gave me the full communist line on religion, and as he moved along he became rather animated. He leaned across the table and continued, "I want you to know that I am an atheist by conviction." Suddenly he stopped. "Oh," he said, "I am sorry. I didn't mean to get so excited!"

I replied, "I am thankful that you have spoken as you have, for I would far sooner talk to a man who speaks what he thinks than to one who evades the issues." And then I leaned across the table and said in a quiet but firm voice, "Now I would like you to know that I am a Christian by *conviction*."

After this exchange we had a very friendly conversation. It seemed as though the Minister relaxed after his awkward effort to missionize for the party.

One of the questions that had to be faced soon after Helsinki was the matter of where the next assembly should be held. We had met two times in Scandinavian countries, once in West Germany, and once in America. It seemed as though it was Germany's turn to play host again. We posed this possibility for the German National Committee. They gave it consideration and came back to suggest that the four member churches in East Germany ought to sponsor the assembly. They emphasized that they knew this would provide a great deal of encouragement to the people of East Germany.

In our consultation with the member churches in East Germany they responded most favorably. They suggested that we should meet in Weimar, in the heart of Luther country. But it was exceedingly important for us to ascertain whether the government would grant the necessary freedom for conducting an LWF assembly. We asked the staff to conduct the conversations with the government. Dr. Appel, the General Secretary for the LWF, and I would be back six months later to check with them on the concessions the government would make.

We reminded the staff that in previous assemblies we had the assurance that any certified delegate would be given a visa, and that materials we needed for reports to the delegates and for the conduct of discussion groups would be admitted without interference. And there had been no censorship or meddling with our news releases. We told our staff that we would have to have the government's promise that such privileges would be granted the assembly if we were to meet in Weimar.

When Dr. Appel and I returned in March, we found that the staff had received verbal assurances on the privileges that had been sought. But we felt that something more solid than verbal commitments were needed. And so we went on to East Berlin to meet with Mr. Seigewasser, the official whose responsibility it was to deal with church relationships.

We had an interesting conversation with Mr. Seigewasser, and he confirmed the report that we had received through our staff. We expressed our joy in this promise. Then I said, "Mr. Seigewasser, I am not happy about telling you this, but there are some people in our churches in the West that say you can't depend on an Eastern European government's word. Would it be possible for you to give us a letter wherein you briefly acknowledge what our understandings are?"

He replied, "Oh, that might be difficult." We talked some more. Suddenly he turned to me and said, "Man, don't you have any faith?"

I replied, "I have faith, but there are many of our people who have reason to know that you cannot always depend on the word of a communist government." I knew that he was eager to have us make the public announcement of our decision to meet in Weimar. And so I said, "I can't make any news release on this until we have some sign that we may show to our people in the West."

Finally Mr. Seigewasser said, "I can't give this promise to you —that decision will have to be made by someone who is higher in government than I." He intimated that the man who would have to pass on it was not in Berlin at the time. I asked when he could have an answer. To provide plenty of time for him to clear with his authority, I suggested that he try to have an answer by May 1. He would not promise that he could have the answer by then, but he would try. I then relented and said, "On your promise that you will try to have the necessary word by May 1, I am ready to go through with our agreement about a press release."

We talked about the day that the release should be made. After this had been determined we agreed that he would make the release in East Berlin and I would make it in West Berlin. The hour of the announcement would be the same for both of us.

After this conversation with Mr. Seigewasser, Dr. Appel and I went across to West Berlin. When we arrived there, we found that EKID (the all Protestant organization) was holding a convention. When I announced to them that the LWF was going to hold its next world assembly in Weimar in East Germany, they stamped their feet with great enthusiasm (their habit instead of clapping their hands). This expressed enthusiasm was followed by spoken words of thanks; they assured us that this would be a morale builder in all of Germany.

After this Dr. Appel and I made it a point of getting the reaction of church and government leaders in different parts of West Germany. Bishop Dibelius in Berlin sent word that he would like us to call on him. He gave us his reaction at once to our decision to meet in Weimar. He said, "This is risky business, but I trust the LWF. Had it been some other ecumenical organization I would not have trusted them to go into communist territory. It might mute their Christian witness." But he gave the LWF his blessing.

Before leaving Berlin we called on Willy Brandt who was then mayor of Berlin. He too thought that our decision was for the good. From Berlin we went to Hamburg. There we had a meeting with the mayor who agreed with our decision. Then we moved into Hanover where the president gave a dinner for us. I am sure that this was at Bishop Lilje's instigation. The president also thought we had taken the right action. From Hanover we traveled into Bavaria. The mayor of Munich gave a dinner for us as did also the president of Bavaria. Both of these officers expressed pleasure at our choice to meet in Weimar. In Württemberg the Prime Minister was not at home, but his deputy invited us for lunch. He seconded the approval that other government leaders had given to the LWF's plan to meet in Weimar.

Our final stopping place in this series of calls was Bonn, Germany's national capital. The government had arranged for a tea to which representatives of various offices in the government, from the university, and from the churches were invited. Among the guests was the former chancellor, Konrad Adenauer. When I shook hands with him and looked into his face, I could understand why he was called "The Fox." There were lines in his face that supported his reputation for being a wise and courageous leader.

Later in the afternoon Prime Minister Erhard invited us to a dinner where cabinet members were present as was the American ambassador. The conversation around the table concerned the decision to hold the next assembly in Weimar in East Germany. There were a number of critical questions. We listened attentively. Thereafter I explained in some detail that the church's primary concern must be for the proclamation of the gospel, whatever the area might be.

All the time that I was talking my ambassador sat across the table shaking his head negatively. After we got through with the dinner, custom decreed that we go into the lounge for coffee. Between my leaving the dinner table and getting into the lounge, the chaplain had talked to Erhard. After I got into the lounge Erhard came over to me and gently nudged me over to a corner where there was a small sofa. We sat down and others joined us standing around us with their coffee cups. Mr. Schroeder, the foreign minister, was one of these as was the American ambassador.

I repeated and enlarged upon what I had said at the table. Mr. Erhard replied, "You are right. The church is the servant of peace, and it must be ready to go to all people. Then after a little more small talk, we got up, and before long the dinner party was over. The American ambassador came to me and asked, "Could we have lunch together tomorrow?" I said, "I am sorry, I have to leave the first thing in the morning." He replied, "Could you give me the names of some books through which I might get better informed about the Lutheran Church?" I answered, "I will do better than that. I'll send you some books when I get back home."

I sent the ambassador several books when I returned to the States. A letter went out under separate cover. I tried to paraphrase the truths he might look for in the books. But I felt I must say more. I wanted him to be aware that I saw the negative nod of his head while I was speaking at Mr. Erhard's dinner. He made no reply, but his actions in subsequent contacts were worth more than any apology.

The letter that Mr. Seigewasser had promised to try to have in our hands by May 1 did not arrive. I wrote to General Secretary Appel that he should notify Mr. Seigewasser that our executive committee would be meeting in Belgrade in July. I asked Appel to advise him that if we had no letter from him by that time we would have to cancel our plans to hold the assembly in Weimar.

The letter had not arrived when the executive committee met. On the first day Appel and I reviewed for them what had transpired. Two members of the committee who were from East Germany said they hoped we would not have to take the initiative in cancelling the plans for Weimar. If we were to do this, it would open the way for the East German government to say to the churches and to the general public—"We offered them the use of our university and its dormitories. On the campus there would be no one to interfere with their meetings. We really extended ourselves to be hospitable." The two East German committee members said that a news release such as this would be a heavy blow for the churches.

But the Lord provided a way out. The morning after our discussion a telegram was received from Mr. Seigewasser. He said, "Because of the policies of certain churchmen in West Germany, we have found it necessary to cancel the invitation to meet in Weimar."

The telegram from Mr. Seigewasser turned the thoughts of the executive committee once more to finding a host for the next assembly. We were eager that it might be on some other continent than Europe or North America. We turned to one of the committee members who was from Brazil, Dr. Gottschald. He was the president of the Evangelical Lutheran Church of the Augsburg Confession in that country. We inquired whether his church might be able to host the assembly. He promised that he would take it up with his church council.

Before long an invitation was at hand from Dr. Gottschald. Dr. Appel went down to Porto Alegre, where the church had its offices. He visited with the church council and with the government representatives to ascertain whether we could enjoy the freedom to hold a good assembly. Appel's report was favorable and so we began aiming for an assembly in Brazil in the summer of 1970.

But once again our plans were aborted. In 1964 a military government came into power in Brazil. Under this government some critical things occurred, especially in northeastern Brazil where there was much abject poverty. The Roman Catholic bishop, Dom Helder Camara, had carried on a great work for the poor. In doing this there were some instances where government had been criticized for providing no poverty alleviation for the poor. This criticism resulted in some arrests and a careful watch was placed on those who were associated with the church's work.

These things were written about in Europe and North America. Mounting criticism of the Brazilian government was happening in all parts of the world.

The executive committee of the LWF met in Copenhagen in December 1969. We reviewed our decision to meet in Brazil. It was acknowledged that there were many unsavory things in the conduct of the government. But were they enough to set aside the host church's desire that we meet in Porto Alegre? The executive committee voted that we stay by our commitment. After this session Archbishop Simojoki of Finland, our first vice-president, said to me, "I stand solidly by your side," meaning on the decision we had made to remain in Brazil.

Despite the decision to remain with the plan to meet in Brazil, the executive committee sensed that we might encounter a change that would compel us to meet somewhere else. And since the time for the next assembly was only eight months away, if there were to be a change there would have to be decisive action. They therefore authorized the officers of the Federation to make whatever decision they thought wise in such an emergency.

Dr. Appel went down to Porto Alegre to check out the physical provisions for our session and to probe the government's attitude. The host church insisted that a government officer be invited to greet the assembly. Normally, this would have been welcomed. But with what had been happening in Brazil, many voices would have protested that to grant such permission would be the equivalent of an LWF endorsement of the Brazilian government's actions. And so we had to decline this proposal of the host church.

In the early spring of 1970 so many protests came in from member churches on the plan to meet in Brazil that I had to call a meeting of the officers. I invited the department heads to sit with us in this consultation. Then each person in the meeting was asked to state his opinion of what action he thought we should take. This resulted in a consensus that we remain in Brazil. It was only four months before this that the executive committee had reconfirmed the acceptance of the Porto Alegre invitation.

Brazil? No!—Evian, France? Yes!

Not long after this consultation of the officers Dr. Appel telephoned me and reached me on a Sunday morning in Mason City, Iowa. He reported that it was almost certain that East Germany would not allow their delegates to go to Brazil. Archbishop Simojoki, who had told me at Copenhagen in December, "I stand solidly by your side" had informed Appel that he would not be coming if we met in Brazil. (Later, he told me that if we were to meet there and if he were to go, he would not be able to work with his young people any longer.) A West German bishop had reported that he would not be coming. The bishops of the Scandinavian countries had met and were agreed that they would be repudiated by many of their people if they were to go. It looked as though we might have a rump assembly. The older member churches who made the larger gifts for the Federation's work would be absent from participating in the important decisions on budget. While the Third World churches would likely attend, they would feel ill at ease with so many leaders absent.

I said to Dr. Appel, "We must change our plans at once. But the assembly must go on. Get in touch with the proper agency in Geneva. You have full authority to go ahead and arrange for holding the assembly at any place in Europe where we can get the facilities we need."

It wasn't many days before Appel got back to me with the news that we would be meeting at Evian in France. It is a resort community with plenty of accommodations. And since Evian is not too far from Geneva, the heavy load for the staff with a minimum amount of time was made tolerable.

I must record two significant items that are associated with the assembly at Evian—regarding youth participation in the assembly and ecumenical relations.

In previous assemblies youth had attended as visitors and observers. I proposed to the executive committee that for the Fifth Assembly we should assign spaces for youth in the delegate quotas. But this would be reckoned over and above a church's regular quota of delegates. There was some hesitance about voting approval. The matter was therefore referred to a committee for evaluation. Bishop Lilje served as the committee's chairman. When it was time for the committee to report, the chairman moved approval. He spoke strongly for it. He asserted that the spaces assigned to the youth should be accorded full delegate status. And this was voted.

At the assembly the youth almost wore out their welcome. The first few days during plenary sessions they called for the floor frequently, most of the time to make some criticism. One evening they brought in a coffin-like box. The LWF was supposed to be the body in the coffin. Another evening they made a bonfire with LWF mimeographed reports. Through this action they wanted to testify that in their judgment the federation was preoccupied with paper work.

The youth appeared frequently before the resolutions committee. The resolutions they offered sought to unload the problems of the Third World countries on the nations of the West. Fortunately, Dr. Paul Empie was chairman of the resolutions committee. His great patience and depth of knowledge about international affairs registered with the young people. They complained to him that LWF resolutions regarding affairs in the Third World failed to identify the nations of the West which, in their judgment, should be held accountable for their poverty. Dr. Empie reminded them that if this were to be done—all nations that had anything to do with the Third World would have to be named. Russia and her satellite countries would also have to be mentioned. This comment immediately quieted the waters, and there was no longer any disposition to press for their partisan critical emphases.

During a coffee break, a young man from Sweden came to me and said, "I suppose you will never again support the presence of youth as delegates in an LWF assembly."

I replied, "Indeed I would. I have not given up on you because of the things that have happened in this assembly; but I don't think that you have used your time and opportunities wisely." He smiled, and as he walked away I sensed that a bond of fellowship had been established.

The Evian Assembly registered a high water mark in the recognition that the body of Christ is one. Through the activity of Professor Kristian Skydsgaard, Cardinal Willebrands, the head of the congregation on Christian Unity in Rome, participated in the assembly program. He gave a plenary session address that warmed the hearts of all the delegates. One could paraphrase what he said about Luther with the statement, "Luther belongs to all of us."

This chapter has been called "The Lutheran Church and Global Relationships." The point has been that the LWC and its successor, the LWF, have shown that we are a global family. Dr. Abdel Ross Wentz was a church historian of stature and he was one of the early leaders in Lutheran cooperation. Editor Bodensieck asked him to write the story of the LWF for the *Encyclopedia of the Lutheran Church*. He concludes that story with this revealing observation:

In summary, the Federation has led the Lutherans of the world to lift their eyes above the limitations of language and nationality and ecclesiastical organization. It has brought them closer to unified intelligence and the consciousness of solidarity than they have ever been before in the four centuries of their history. And it has enabled them to present a more effective witness to their common faith.

9

THE REALITY OF THE HOLY CHRISTIAN CHURCH

FOR YEARS ON END LUTHERANS HAVE asserted the *reality* of the holy Christian Church in their weekly Sunday confession of the Third Article in the Apostles' Creed. Peruse this article of faith and ask yourself whether you can find any other meaning in the Third Article?

> I believe in the Holy Spirit,
> the holy Christian Church,
> the communion of saints,
> the forgiveness of sins,
> the resurrection of the body,
> and the life everlasting. Amen.

Despite the obvious meaning of our confession we have had great difficulty investing this truth in our daily contact with other churches. This is particularly true in our relation with the Roman

Catholic Church. Let me illustrate this observation by some experiences in my own life.

I was in the fourth grade when the Roman Catholic parish in our town built a school building. When this took place there were a number of Catholic children that withdrew from the public school in order to register in their parish school. Among them were a couple of boys who were part of a group with whom I had been associating.

I did not like to see them leave. I expressed my regret to one of the boys. He took the occasion to lecture me about being a Lutheran. Didn't I know that the Roman Catholic Church was the *true* church of Christ?

My experience as a boy, and even at St. Olaf College, provided me no special opportunity for bridging the gap between the Lutheran and Roman Catholic churches. But in my second parish, Trinity in Moorhead, a contact developed that became the beginning of a new attitude toward the Catholic church. It was during the time of the depression years in the early '30s. The local Chamber of Commerce organized a community committee to assist people who were lacking in the ordinary needs for sustenance. The Roman Catholic priest, Father Lambert, and I were asked to serve as counselors for the committee.

Since Father Lambert did not have a car, I called for him before each meeting. When I took him home, we would often sit in the car visiting at some length. Our discussions were usually theological. I sensed a good deal of identity in our understanding of Scripture's basic teachings. In the process of these visits I learned to respect and love Father Lambert.

This, and other later experiences with Roman Catholic people, led me to believe that there ought to be a planned opportunity for heads of Protestant churches to meet with Roman bishops for fellowship and theological exchange. It seemed to me that the Executive Director of the National Council of Churches in America (NCCA) would be the appropriate person to initiate such a project. I made the proposal while participating in a small group meeting in New York where Ed Espy, then the Executive Director of NCCA, was present. Dr. Espy is an evangelically minded man with a good fund of Christian love to invest in ecumenical relations.

But Dr. Espy turned the proposal about. He insisted that I should call the meeting—probably because at that time I was president of the ALC. This was a turn in the road I had not expected. The men in the group meeting strongly supported Ed's suggestion. What could I do? I believed the impulse to seek such informal fellowship was of God, and so I had to yield to their importunities.

The first meeting was called by sending a letter of invitation to the head of each major Protestant body. It was carefully explained that participation in the proposed groups would be on a voluntary basis (not an official meeting). Each would have to pay his own expenses. Meetings would probably be annual and certainly not more than twice a year. The meetings would be held in different parts of the country. Invitations to Roman Catholic bishops would be through the counsel of the appropriate Catholic leaders.

It is my recollection that our second meeting was held in Seattle. During a discussion seeking to identify basic emphases in the Christian faith, a young priest by the name of William Baum, who was then serving in Seattle, participated in the discussion with evangelical enthusiasm. At one point he turned to me as though I might be representing all Lutherans and said, "You Lutherans, don't ever, don't ever give up your emphasis on justification by faith!"

I had never thought that a Roman Catholic priest would make such a statement. Since then Father Baum has been archbishop of the Archdiocese of Washington; in 1976 he was made cardinal by Pope Paul VI, and recently was named by Pope John Paul to head the Vatican group that supervises Catholic seminaries and universities around the world.

It became increasingly clear that Pope John XXIII's call for the Second Vatican Council was the expression of an initiative by the Holy Spirit. There were Lutheran theologians that helped the church to recognize what was taking place. Among these I mention two names: Bishop Hermann Dietzfelbinger of the Bavarian Evangelical Lutheran Church and Professor Kristian Skydsgaard of the University of Copenhagen.

At the LWF Assembly in Minneapolis in 1957 Bishop Dietzfelbinger came to the preassembly meeting of the Executive Committee with a proposal that we set up a special committee to study the whole question of relations with the Roman Catholic Church. He said there had been a great improvement in relations with the Roman church in Bavaria. And he felt that it was time that we be alert to what the Lord of the Church might be saying.

A few in the Executive Committee were afraid that our people might misunderstand. In response to some of the doubts I remember saying in the Executive Committee, "God's Spirit may be speaking to us through Bishop Dietzfelbinger's proposal. And we should not overlook the fact that it was supported by the entire German National Committee." The proposal then went to the assembly with the recommendation of the Executive Committee, and the assembly approved it.

The study committee reported to the Helsinki Assembly in 1963 recommending that we set up an ecumenical institute. To begin with the intent was that we devote attention to Roman Catholic theology, but later it was enlarged so that other areas could be included. Helsinki authorized the organization of a Lutheran Foundation for Inter-Confessional Research.

After this authorization the Executive Committee wrestled with the question of where this institute should be located. Some thought it ought to be located in Geneva. And others thought it should be Copenhagen, a central place as far as all European

Lutheranism was concerned. It was finally agreed that it should be established at Strasbourg in France; there it would be in the midst of strong Lutheran and Roman Catholic parishes.

One of the moving spirits in the support of Bishop Dietzfelbinger was Dr. Skydsgaard. He became the first chairman for the Foundation board. Professor Skydsgaard is an irenic person, a real apostle of love. And he probably knows more about Roman Catholic theology than any other Lutheran theologian. He has been a guest lecturer in a number of Roman seminars. On such occasions students have frequently sought him out to get the Lutheran position on some current theological issues. As the result of the work of these two men and the many supporting theologians in the Federation member churches, a new awareness of the meaning of the church had been released. The primary emphasis was on the church as the Body of Christ rather than as organization.

At the Evian Assembly in 1970 we had the privilege of having Cardinal Jan Willebrands as one of the program participants. I knew that Cardinal Willebrands would not have been at our Federation Assembly without the approval of the Pope. It seemed therefore that a word of thanks should be relayed to him. This thought gripped me during an assignment that would take me through Rome while the Second Vatican Council was in session. I conferred with a WCC officer in this field, asking whether it would be appropriate for me to seek permission to sit in on the Vatican Council sessions as an observer for a few hours. He answered, "Oh, indeed!" He volunteered to make the arrangements for me, but, he said, "You would then have to seek an audience with the Pope. It would be counted a discourtesy if the LWF president were in attendance at the assembly and did not do this." I thanked him for his counsel but could not give an immediate yes to his offer to help make the arrangements.

I felt that as far as the Americans were concerned there would be a strong tendency to misunderstand. But it might be different among the European Lutherans. I turned to Bishop Lilje and inquired, "How would your people in Germany feel if it were announced that I was having an audience with Pope Paul?" He said, "Oh, that would be misunderstood and misinterpreted." I said, "That settles it for me." And so I advised my friend in the WCC office in Geneva that I would merely change planes in Rome and follow my itinerary.

However, a new turn in the road occurred. In January of 1971 I was in Addis Ababa at a meeting of the Central Committee of the WCC. The Roman Catholic Church had two official visitors of their Congregation on Christian Unity in attendance. In conversations with these two men and with WCC member church delegates it was clear that a new spirit of trust was emerging in relationships with the Roman church.

One day when I was in conversation with the two Roman representatives and they discovered that I had had thoughts of stopping off in Rome to express the Federation's gratitude for Cardinal Willebrands' attendance at our Evian Assembly, they immediately insisted that I allow them to set up an appointment for me with the Pope. I had heard and seen enough to feel that men like Skydsgaard and Dietzfelbinger were reading the new story on relationships with Rome truthfully. I therefore accepted their proffered offer to arrange the audience.

When I came to Rome I was met by Father Hasler, who had been one of the Roman men in the dialog with the Lutherans. He greeted me with the words, "I am happy that you have come to express the gratitude of the LWF, for there were some who were critical of the Pope for his permitting Cardinal Willibrands to go to your Evian Assembly. And when they heard what he had said they were still more critical. It will be good for the Pope to hear your expression of thanks."

I had not expected to spend more than ten minutes in the audience with the Pope. After all, it doesn't take long to say

"Thanks." But the Pope kept me there for 35 minutes. He initiated the conversation by saying, "I want you to know that our church puts a strong emphasis on the use of the Bible, in the church and in the homes of the people." Some cynic could say that he knew that was a good thing to say to a Lutheran. But I studied his face as he talked, and his features reflected a man who was speaking out of an honest heart. And I was fully aware of the report in ecumenical circles that today some of the best Bible interpreters are from Rome.

After the Pope's Bible statement, he shifted ground and said, "Of course we take a severe position on all morality." This seemed to suggest that he was leading up to something specific. I did not think that it would be abortion, although he may have had that in mind; but at the time it was not under as much discussion as was population control. And I felt that lest he misunderstand because I had agreed with him so heartily on several things he had said, I interrupted with the observation, "But our church cannot support your position on population control. We believe that Christian parents have an obligation to bring children into the world unless health conditions interfere. However, in a day when there is an overpopulation in many parts of the world, the command 'Be fruitful and multiply' carries a different meaning than it did in Adam's day."

He became very quiet, almost pensive, and then he said, "It's clear that this needs more study." When he said this, it seemed to me that I saw the Pope as not only the spiritual head of the church but also as administrator, the administrator that had to keep the family together. It is generally known that they have had a commission studying this issue for a considerable length of time.

As we were to take leave of one another, he presented me with a couple of gifts. I took his right hand in speaking my thanks and a word of farewell. He then placed his left hand over our clasped hands thus holding my right hand between his two hands. In doing this he said, "Pray for us." I replied, "I prayed for you this morning." Then with a big smile he added, "Come and see us again."

Postscript

This is the story of a man who as a boy had his heart on missionary work in China, but whose course was deflected by the revolutions in Asia. Before his career was ended, his path had criss-crossed continents and his service to the missionary enterprise and to world Christendom could not possibly have been predicted when in 1930 he became a pastor in Duluth, Minnesota.

One cannot read the book without a feeling that step by step he walked through doors that opened to him, satisfied at any time to be doing what was then at hand. The doors opened on an ecclesiastical world ready for ecumenical understanding, and he, by temperament and conviction, was ready to enter with the gifts which the Lord had given him from birth.

Alvin N. Rogness